GLOBALISATION AND DEVELOPMENT OF BACKWARD AREAS

GLOBALISATION AND DEVELOPMENT OF BACKWARD AREAS

Edited by
G. Satyanarayana

Department of Economics and Applied Economics,
Sri Krishnadevaraya University,
Anantapur

in association with

New Century Publications
New Delhi, India

NEW CENTURY PUBLICATIONS
4800/24, Bharat Ram Road,
Ansari Road, Daryaganj,
New Delhi - 110 002

Tel.: 23247798, 65396605
Telefax: 011- 41017798
E-mail: indiatax@vsnl.com
www.newcenturypublications.com

Editorial office:
34, Gujranwala Town, Part-2,
Delhi - 110 009
Tel.: 27247805, 27464774

First Published - June 2007

ISBN: 81-7708-149-7 (*10 digit*)
978-81-7708-149-7 (*13 digit*)

Published by New Century Publications and printed at Singhal Print Media, New Delhi -110 005

PRINTED IN INDIA

Dedicated to

Bhagawan Sri Venkaiah Swamy

Ph.Nos.08554 – 255231 (O), 255267 (R)
Fax : 08554 – 255244 / 255295
E-mail : vcatpsku@yahoo.com

**SRI KRISHNADEVARAYA UNIVERSITY
ANANTAPUR**

From

PROF. RAMARA ATHOTA *M.Sc., Ph.D.*,
VICE-CHANCELLOR

19th April,2007

FOREWORD

Although India's development has been quite satisfactory during the post-Independence period yet inter-State and intra-State disparities in the standard of living are a stark reality. Owing to its vastness, the country exhibits heterogeneity and therefore specific problems of each backward area need to be studied in depth for strategic solutions. An attempt has been made in this direction by Professor G. Satyanarayana as editor of the present book which consists 25 research articles, authored by experienced academicians and researchers, spelling out strategies for the development of backward regions with focus on drought prone district Anantapur in Andhra Pradesh. This book would appeal to all those who feel concerned about the plight of poor people in backward areas of the country. It provides useful reference material for government functionaries, legislators, NGOs and the general readers interested in the development of backward regions. The book covers a wide range of subjects including Globalisation, Environment, Agriculture, Industry, Women Empowerment, Tourism, and Infrastructure Development. I wish that this book receives all the patronage that it richly deserves.

(Rama Rao Athota)
Vice-Chancellor
Sri Krishnadevaraya University
Ananapur, Andhra Pradesh, India

About the Book

Globalisation is widely seen as the most important factor that could influence economies of nations the world over in the new millennium. The rapid advancement in information technology and communications has made it not just possible but absolutely essential for industry the world over to adapt or fall by the wayside.

The most important aspects of economic globalisation are:

- breaking down of national barriers;
- international spread of trade, financial and production activities, and
- growing power of transnational corporations and international financial institutions in these processes.

While economic globalisation is a very uneven process, with increased trade and investment being focused in a few countries,

The issue that concerns developing countries is how one can ensure greater participation of the weaker economies, particularly backward regions of these economies, in the global process and what needs to be done to ensure that the course of globalisation benefits more people in more countries.

The socio-economically disadvantaged are yet to benefit from reform policies. The challenge to overcome the scourge of poverty remains a daunting task. The support of the poor for reforms, and their involvement in the development process can be achieved only if they start benefiting from the policies. It is necessary to ensure that the poor and the deprived have an even greater stake in economic reforms than at present for mobilising their enthusiastic participation in the development process. Economic reforms must be guided by compassion and distributive justice. Improvement of living conditions of the poorest and the weakest sections of society should be high priority areas in the first decade of the new millennium.

This book analyses the trend towards globalisation and focuses on implications of it for backward regions of India.

Editor's Profile

Dr. G. Satyanarayana is professor and presently the Chairman of the Board of Studies in the Department of Economics and Applied Economics, Sri Krishnadevaraya University, Anantapur, Andhra Pradesh. A gold medalist in M.A. (Economics), he got his M.Phil. and Ph.D. Degrees in Economics from Sri Krishnadevaraya University. He has published one book and more than 60 research papers in various journals of repute. He has successfully completed one major research project funded by the University Grants Commission (UGC), New Delhi. Under his research supervision, 19 Ph.D. degrees and 13 M.Phil. degrees in economics have been awarded so far. He has worked extensively on small-scale and cottage industries in the backward areas of the State of Andhra Pradesh..

Editor's Note on the Book

Globalisation implies widening and deepening integration with the *globe*, i.e. with people and processes abroad. The trend towards the evolution of a global society is generally thought of in economic terms and in terms of the consequences of the revolution in communication technologies. There is undoubtedly much greater economic integration among the nations of the world today.

Globalisation is widely seen as the most important factor that could influence economies of nations the world over in the new millennium. The rapid advancement in information technology and communications has made it not just possible but absolutely essential for industry the world over to adapt or fall by the wayside.

The 1990s witnessed a paradigm shift towards market-oriented economic policies and a careful dismantling of obstacles in its wake. This has helped the smaller, emerging economies gain access to world markets, emergent technologies and collaborations. This has also given them a window to the developed world and helped them understand the significant role of globalisation as an instrument, which could be utilised not just to achieve economic efficiency, but also eradicate poverty.

Globalisation has also resulted in the creation of a new business framework. More changes can be expected in the business scenario specifically in terms of openness, adaptiveness and responsiveness.

The most important aspects of economic globalisation are:

- breaking down of national barriers;
- international spread of trade, financial and production activities, and
- growing power of transnational corporations and international financial institutions in these processes.

While economic globalisation is a very uneven process, with increased trade and investment being focused in a few countries, almost all countries are greatly affected by this process.

A major feature of globalisation is the growing concentration and monopolisation of economic resources and power by transnational corporations and by global financial firms and funds. This process has been termed transnationalisation, in which fewer and fewer transnational corporations are gaining a large and rapidly increasing proportion of world economic resources, production and market shares. Where a multinational company used to dominate the market of a single product, a big transnational company now typically produces or trades in an increasing multitude of products, services and sectors. Through mergers and acquisitions, fewer and fewer of these TNCs now control a larger and larger share of the global market, whether in commodities, manufactures or services.

A unique feature of the current globalisation process is the globalisation of national policies and policy-making mechanism. National policies (including economic, social, cultural and technological areas) that until recently were determined by the States and people within a country have increasingly come under the influence of international agencies and processes or by big private corporations and economic/financial players. This has led to the narrowed ability of governments and people to make choices from options in economic, social and cultural policies.

Most developing countries have seen their independent policy-making mechanism capacity eroded, and have to adopt policies influenced by other entities, which may on balance be detrimental to the countries concerned. The developed countries, where the major economic players reside, and which also control the processes and policies of international economic agencies, are better able to maintain control over their own national policies as well as determine the policies and practices of international institutions and the global system. However, it is also true that the large corporations have taken over a large part of decision-making even in the developed countries, at the expense of the power of the State or political and social leaders.

However, at the end of the day, one has to understand and accept that globalisation is the stratagem for the new millennium.

Every country, developed and developing, has to accept this and formulate their economies around it. The issue that concerns developing countries is how one can ensure greater participation of the weaker economies, particularly backward regions of these economies, in the global process and what needs to be done to ensure that the course of globalisation benefits more people in more countries.

The uneven and unequal nature of the present globalisation is manifested in the fast growing gap between the world's rich and poor people and between developed and developing countries; and by the large differences among nations in the distribution of gains and losses.

This imbalance leads to polarisation between countries and groups that gain, and countries and groups that lose out or are marginalised. Globalisation, polarisation, wealth concentration and marginalisation are therefore linked through the same process. In this process, investment resources, growth and modern technology are focused on a few countries, mainly in North America, Europe, Japan and a few East Asian countries. A majority of developing countries are excluded from the process, or are participating in it in marginal ways.

Although the developed world is in a dominant position and has been prepared to use this to further their control of the global economy, the developing countries have not done well in organising themselves to co-ordinate on substantial policy and negotiating positions. The developed countries, on the other hand, are well organised within their own countries, with well-staffed departments dealing with international trade and finance, and with university academics and private and quasi-government think tanks helping to obtain information and map policies and strategies. They also have well-organised associations and lobbies associated with their corporations and financial institutions, which have great influence over the government departments.

Globalisation is an irreversible trend and developing economies are also inevitably involved in the process. One should therefore, carefully consider how to restructure the world trading system to accommodate developing economies, by enabling them to benefit from globalisation while minimising external shocks. The World Trade Organisation (WTO) should work more effectively, through an enlargement of waiver clauses which recognise the weaker position of developing countries.

On the positive side, globalisation has compelled developing countries to improve overall economic management, and make their economies efficient. To get a share of global capital and technology, developing countries have to upgrade their social and economic institutions through administrative, legislative and legal reforms. The quality of governance has to improve to encourage productivity and efficiency. Political stability has to be established. If we were to draw lessons from the East Asian countries, we would get several valuable insights: (i) developing human capital is a basic pre-requisite. Successful globalisation and the knowledge economy require educated, healthy and skilled people; (ii) it is necessary to build up domestic savings and put it to productive use; (iii) sound economic management and macro-economic balances are necessary. Large fiscal deficit is a serious obstacle to globalisation; (iv) good governance at the national and sub-national level builds confidence among investors; (v) transparency has to be established in the functioning of both government and business units; (vi) free and open market economies require effective regulatory authorities, as government's role changes from control and regulation to governance and facilitation; (vii) modernised capital markets with effective regulatory authorities to impart confidence to investors by maintaining stability and regulating speculative forces.

The socio-economically disadvantaged are yet to benefit from reform policies. The challenge to overcome the scourge of poverty remains a daunting task. The support of the poor for reforms, and their involvement in the development process can be achieved only if they start benefiting from the policies. It is necessary to ensure that the poor and the deprived have an even greater stake in economic reforms than at present for mobilising their enthusiastic participation in the development process.

Economic reforms must be guided by compassion and distributive justice. Improvement of living conditions of the poorest and the weakest sections of society should be high priority areas in the first decade of the new millennium.

Despite such distortions and aberrations, globalisation is a reality. Developments in information and communication technologies will unify markets and people, cutting across barriers of space and time.

This book analyses the trend towards globalisation and focuses on implications of it for backward regions of India. It consists of 25 papers authored by scholars in the field. I place on record my deep appreciation and gratefulness to each of them for their worthy contributions.

I profusely thank Professor M.L. Kantha Rao, my teacher and research supervisor, who inspired me undertake this task for wider debate among academicians and policy-makers.

June 21, 2007 G. Satyanarayana
Anantapur

List of Contributors

G. SATYANARAYANA	Chairman, Board of Studies, Department of Economics and Applied Econometrics, Sri Krishnadevaraya University, Anantapur.
M. REDDI RAMU	Research Scholar, Sri Krishnadevaraya University, Anantapur.
Y. KESAVA REDDY	Assistant Professor, Intell Engineering College, Anantapur.
M.V. RAGHAVULU	Senior Lecturer in Economics, Government First Grade Degree College, Bellary.
A. RAMA MOHANA	Research Scholar, Department of Economics, Sri Krishnadevaraya University, Anantapur.
M.L. KANTHA RAO	Formerly Member, Andhra Pradesh Public Service Commission, Hyderabad.
I. SREENIVASULU	Technical Officer, Andhra Pradesh Industrial Technical Consultancy Organisation, Hyderabad.
B. VIJAYA LAKSHMI	Senior Grade Lecturer in Economics, Government Degree College, Anantapur.

Contents

Part I: Globalisation and Socio-economic Concerns

By
G. Satyanarayana
M. Reddi Ramu
Y. Kesava Reddy
M.V. Raghavulu
A. Rama Mohana

1

Rural Development Strategies in India

This article has been presented in two parts: Part A deals with the theoretical aspects of globalisation and Part B is devoted to rural development strategies in India in the context of globalisation.

Part A

The Globalisation ideology is based on the idea that more and more production and consumption of output alone is a substantial and major source form of human happiness. Globalisation denotes an economic process of integrating country's economy with the world economy, through free enterprise and free trade. It propagates global capitalist development process as a way out for moving towards further heights in creating prosperity through which global poverty and inequalities may be addressed efficiently. This is a tall claim of the proponents of the globalisation process.

In the Indian context of globalisation implies relaxation of restrictions on participation of foreign direct investment, multinational corporations and foreign collaborations and liberalization of imports and exports. The thrust to globalisation has been provided since the new IPR and Trade policies of Indian in July 1991.

Globalisation in India continues to be subject to the democratic process.

Globalisation process is based on the following premises:

1. Maximization of economic efficiency.
2. Increasing factor productivity and realizing more and more economies of scale and range.
3. Augmentation of supply of factors of production.
4. Use of modern technology and organization abilities to

enhance the production capabilities.

5. Creation and augmentation of individual property, economic freedom and individual capabilities.

All the above rolled into one goal: Maximization of economic of growth on sustaining basis.

Potential benefits of globalisation are as under:

1. Reduction in the cost production.
2. Fall-in prices and increase in market access.
3. Realization of economies of scale and range and thus increase in profitability.
4. Increases in global income, output and employment.
5. Increases in World consumption and standards of living and thereby, reduction in world poverty.
6. Global decline in world development gaps in income, consumption and opportunities.
7. Enabling global environment for Trade expansion and widening consumer choice.
8. Economic use of global resources.
9. Decline in gender gaps in development process and benefits.

Disadvantages of globalisation

1. Excessive consumerism resulting in environmental pollution, more emission of green house gases and degradation of natural resources.
2. De-industrialization of newly industrializing countries.
3. Probability of increasing unemployment, under-employment and growing causualisation of labour.
4. Increasing poverty and income inequalities.
5. Widening development gap between rich and poor countries.
6. More threat of feminization of poverty particularly rural women.
7. Globalisation of agriculture causing rural impoverishment and occurrence of droughts and famines.
8. Increasing food insecurity and other forms of life insecurity.
9. Increase in human trafficking owing to the raise of poverty levels.

The Buddhist and Gandhian social and ethical philosophies

alone can reduce the disadvantages of globalisation.

Why Globalisation Works?

Martin wolf has advanced four fundamental strong grounds in defense to say why globalization works. They are:

1. There is for the moment, a single in disputed hegemony – the United States and war among great powers in the near future seems unlikely;
2. All the great powers seem to have abandoned the nation that property derives from the territorial gains and plunder rather than from internal economic development and peaceful exchange;
3. All the great powers now share a commitment to market-led economic development and international economic and political integration of some kind; and
4. Global institutions and close international cooperation reinforce the basic stability of the political order.

Who are the Beneficiaries of Globalisation?

Internationally, globalisation has yielded impressive growth dividends, including for relatively poor countries. The list of 'post-1980 globalizes' includes Argentina, Brazil, China, Hungary, Malaysia, Mexico, the Philippines and Thailand which as a group, experienced an acceleration in average growth from 1.6 per annum in 1960's to 2.9 per cent per annum in the 1970's 3.5 per cent per annum in 1980's and 5 per cent in the 1990's.

Five years after the WTO came into existence; the anticipated gains from the trade liberalization process in agriculture are particularly non-existent. Since 1996-97 total agricultural exports have declined from US$ 6,828 million to US$ 5,475 million and agricultural imports have increased from US$ 39,132 million to US$ 47,212 million. India, thus exports a very small percentage of its production.

But in India inter-regional disparities have widened during the globalisation period i.e. after 1991.

Are there Threats to Globalisation?

"If the United States remain wedded to nations of global primacy rather than of a shared global order, conflict with a rising China would seem almost inevitable", Wolf cautioned. In addition to these political pressures, China's ascent will force uncomfortable economic adjustment on the rest of the world-a phenomenon that is already fuelling protectionist pressures in a number of countries.

But a great threat to the world's commitment to open borders is mega terrorism. Hence, Wolf called for global cooperation and improved security measures rather than closing borders as a means of controlling terrorists.

The protagonists of globalisation argue that the globalisation policies shall be appropriately designed, and their timely and sequencing and operationalisation shall be rationalized. Then the social costs of globalisation would be invariably lower and fewer than its benefits. It should be remembered, however, that the gaps between promises and reality could be many and very severe. Therefore, the adverse social consequences of globalisation may be tackled through Gandhian instrument of public resistance.

Part B

Globalisation is no longer option; it is a fast as India is one of the members of the club of Globalizes. As such India has followed the policy of globalisation for over decade.

Although geographically India occupies 2.2 per cent of the world area accounting for more than 15 per cent of the world population, its share in the world market is just 0.67 per cent (1999) whereas the China's share in the world market is 3.6 per cent in spite of the fact that it is the number of one country in the world in respect of the highest population.

If one examines India's share in the world exports vis-à-vis china, South Korea and Mexico, the position of India in this aspect has been not significantly improved over a period one decade.

As per the data provided by the World Bank, India's share in world exports increased from 0.54 per cent in 1990 to 0.67 per cent in 1999. Whereas world exports rose by about 64 per cent during 1990 to 1999 (Table 1.1), India exports rose by 103 per cent during the same period. It was 214 per cent, 123 per cent and 236 per cent tin the case of China, South Korea and Mexico.

It is a matter of satisfaction to note that India has enjoyed a unique position with respect exports of services in the world. In fact India stands first among the four countries (Table 1.2) referred above.

India has achieved 203 per cent increase in service exports from 1990 to 1999 while the same has been far less when compared to china, South Korea and Mexico respectively 103 per cent, 171 per cent and 164 per cent. Thus it conclusively proves that globalisation paved a way for supplying skilled man power to many developed countries. This is significantly contributed to improve forest reserves which are around US$ 130 billions in India.

Alternative Strategies for Rural Development in India

Globalisation is the process by which the world economy is transformed from asset of national and regional markets into a set of global markets without regard to national and regional boundaries.

In order to reap the benefits of globalisation, the Government of India has to adopt the following alternative strategies to achieve rural development.

1. Awareness Camps: Globalisation concept and its operation have been largely confined to metropolitan cities in India. District headquarters and smaller urban centres have been not actively engaged in global transactions leave alone rural areas. There is an urgent need for creating awareness among the realties with regard to the concept of globalisation and various other related aspects of globalisation.

2. Change in Cropping Pattern: Farmer are to be educated to put their land other agriculture inputs such as water, power, pesticides, fertilizers, seed and labour force to the optimum

Table 1.1: Merchandise Exports of Selected Countries of the World

Country	Exports US$ million		As per cent of World Exports		%age increase in 1999 over 1990	Annual average growth rate (1990-99)
	1990	1999	1990	1999		
India	17957	36560	0.54	0.67	103.4	8.2
China	62091	195150	1.86	3.59	214.3	13.6
South Korea	65016	144745	1.95	2.66	122.6	9.3
Mexico	40711	136703	1.22	2.51	235.8	14.4
World exports	3328357	5442226	100.0	100.0	63.5	5.6

Source: Compiled and computed from the data provided in World Bank, World Development Indicators (2001).

Table 1.2: Service Exports of Selected Countries of the World

Country	Exports US$ million		As per cent of World Exports		%age increase in 1999 over 1990	Annual average growth rate (1990-99)
	1990	1999	1990	1999		
India	4609	13940	0.60	1.1	202.5	13.1
China	1786	3701	0.23	0.29	107.2	8.4
South Korea	9155	24822	1.19	1.95	171.1	11.7
Mexico	7222	11829	0.94	0.93	163.8	5.6
World exports	766353	1271417	100.0	100.0	65.9	5.8

Source: Compiled and computed from the data provided in World Bank, World Development Indicators (2001).

utilization so as to reap maximum returns from agricultural operations. It calls for suitable cropping pattern, keeping in view of the availability of water resources. Farmers are to be advised to be advised to adopt new cropping pattern of raising vegetables, horticulture crops (fruits flowers) medicinal plants, plants that yield bio-diesel oil seeds, commercial crops and timber yielding plants that need minimum water are to be encouraged in place of traditional food crops whose returns are not only lower compared to the crops listed above but also, often, required more water.

3. Technological Transfer: In order to avail the benefits of globalization farmers need to be equipped with the latest tools and knowledge to work on such as equipment. The latest changes in the agricultural technologies are to be transferred for their effective utilization to maximize agricultural productivity in the rural areas. To accomplish this task officials concerned have to plan in such as way to meet the emerging needs of the farming class. Farmers are to be educated to judiciously use fertilizers, pesticides, insecticides and improved variety of seeds for various corps that farmers raise. It is important that farmer should be educated to select genuine seeds before they take up seedling activity; because a large number of farmers in Andhra Pradesh have reported to have incurred heavy loss on account of fake seeds.

4. High Yielding Varieties (HYV's): The Department of Agriculture has to draw plants to periodically train up farmers in the usage of HYV's with appropriate demonstration of practical classes. The high yielding varieties in the fruit of serious research results of agronomists. The high yielding varieties undoubtedly increases the agricultural yield significantly as is evidenced from the Green Revolution. The utilization of HYV's improves the economic condition of the farmers besides meeting the food requirement in the country.

5. Commercial Crops: Thanks the green revolution for meeting food requirement in the country. The country has been enjoying food security with sufficient buffer stocks in the Food Corporation Godowns. As such now is the time for the farmers to go in for cultivation of commercial crops that enrich their economies. The farmers may take up commercial crops such as arekanut, coconut, coffee tea, beetle leaves, spices, cotton, sugar, pluses, medicinal plants, bio-diesel plants and a vast variety of fruits and flowers. The products of the commercial crops find suitable marketing conditions across the world. The forming community may reap rich dividends by merchandising these in the global markets.

6. Hoarding Facilities: Since India enjoys a rich varied bio-diversity its agriculture products range is very wide. Besides its animal wealth has significantly contributed to be production of dairy products. India ranks 7th in the world in the production of fruits. To commercially benefit from all these advantages appropriate hoarding facilities-chilling plants/centres, to stock and sell them when the marketing conditions are favourable are the need of the hour. The Government has a plan suitably to provide hoarding plants/centres in the mandal Headquarters or in big villages where there is a concentration of large number of farmers. The hoarding centre maintain freshness of the products such as fruits, flowers, vegetables and dairy products and preventing all sorts of likely damages and thus benefits the farmers in the rural areas, enabling them to catch up the global trend in improving their economies.

7. Marketing Facilities: The knowledge with respect to demand for our country's rural products and their prices in the global markets in essentially needed by the farmers in the rural areas. For this purpose the Government may provide urban services in the rural areas-internet facility to confer benefit farmers who engage themselves in global transactions.

8. Skill Development: The rural farm labour needs to be trained up to work with the latest agriculture implements-Tractors, Threshers, Harvesters and sprayers. The skill formation goes a long way in improving the productivity levels globalisation.

9. Rural Industrialization: The approach of the Rural Industrialization needs a through over hauling. The traditional cottage industries such as, pottery, tanning, handlooms, oilganies, are fast vanishing from the scene. Rural Industrialization needs a reorientation in the context of globalisation. Rural Industrialization can be vigoursly up in rural areas where the adequate infrastructural facilities are made available. Rural Industrialization canvass should be such as to cover all variety of industries-small, medium and large scale. The governments should come forward with appropriate package schemes to attract even the most modern industries-software production centres, in rural areas as land and labour are available at relatively cheaper cost.

10. Empowerment of Women: Women hold almost half of the sky in India. As such they cannot be ignored in the process of rural development. Women are to be made empowered through education and employment. They must be trained to overcome their superstitious beliefs so as to participate in the nation-building activity. Women can be made to provide education to rural women. For educated women, richly contribute to democratic and development process in rural India.

Further the educated women, without being hold by any body prefer to adopt nuclear family norms and thus they a key-role in population control thereby they enable to enhance per capital income levels which pave a way for better standard of living conditions in the rural areas of the country.

Conclusion

It is an undisputed fact that in the present days, no country in the world survives independently all by itself and India is no exception as it has already become a member of the club of globalizes. India has chalked out a road map to move fast to attain high rate of growth under globalisation. Given the constrains, Indian economy could not catch up the fast track of economic development as in the case of China. This is because of the fact that so far in India, the impact of globalisation has been restricted only to metropolitan cities, leaving out even smaller cities and district headquarters leave alone rural areas. This is not so in the case of China; every inch of the China's geography is being influenced by globalisation process; hence it has achieved a better development over India. The article concludes by urging the Government of India to create such an environment which facilities the rural people to development trade links to merchandise goods and services with the rest of the world to better their economies and thus push up the status of India among the nations of the world.

References

Ismail Shariff: 'Growing Discontent with Globalisation, World affairs, July-Sept, 2003, Vol.7, No.3.

R. Nagaraj: Foreign Direct Investment in India in the 1990s-Trends and Issues, published in the economic and political weekly, April 26, 2003, pp. 1701-1704.

R.D. Mc Cormick:'10 Myths about Globalisation: Modern Civilisation through Trade to all', Vital Speeches of the Day, November 15, 2000.

Ramesh Chandra: Globalisation Liberalisation Privatisation and Indian Policy, ISM Books, Delhi-110033

2

Impact of Globalisation on Indian Agriculture

Globalisation is a ubiquitous buzzword and can be defined as a process of growing interdependence between all people of this planet. People are linked together economically and socially by trade, investments and governance. Societies all over the world are experiencing the globalisation of more and more aspects of life, but accompanied by the contradictions of growing inequality within and between countries.

The debate on merits of globalisation continues, with one side argument that it raises living standards and the others that it worsens poverty and inequality. Certainly, economic globalisation has led to increased wealth for many in some countries. But it also led to shattering economic crisis, collapse in standard of living, widespread societal and ethnic conflict, social disintegration and greatly increased insecurity for disproportionately large part of the world's population.

Martin Wolf, Associate Editor and Chief Economics Commentator, at the 'Financial Times' offered a robust defense of globalization and upbeat assessment of its prospects. In discussing his new book "why Globalisation Works" he has rebutted claims that globalization undermines sovereignty, weakens democracy, intensifies inequality, favours 'exploitative' multinational corporations, and devastates the environment.

Martin Wolf has conceded that China and India – opponents of economic integration could yet do grave damage. However, he strongly feels that the forces against globalization are not strong enough to cause its (globalization) disintegration as it seemed implausible that global disintegration would collapse, as it had in the interwar years of the early 20th century as a consequence of international rivalries, economic instability, protectionist interests and anti-liberal ideas.

Martin wolf has advanced four fundamental strong grounds in defense to say why globalization works. They are:

1. There is for the moment, a single in disputed hegemon – the United States and war among great powers in the near future seems unlikely;
2. All the great powers seem to have abandoned the nation that property derives from the territorial gains and plunder rather than from internal economic development and peaceful exchange;
3. All the great powers now share a commitment to market-led economic development and international economic and political integration of some kind; and
4. Global institutions and close international cooperation reinforce the basic stability of the political order.

The breakdown of the early 20th century order occurred in large part because of the pressures to accommodate rising powers in the global economic and political order. "If the United States remain wedded to nations of global primacy rather than of a shared global order, conflict with a rising china would seem almost inevitable", wolf cautioned. In addition to these political pressures, China's ascent will force uncomfortable economic adjustment on the rest of the world-a phenomenon that is already fueling protectionist pressures in a number of countries. But a greater threat to the world's commitment to open boarders is mega terrorism.

Hence, wolf called for global co-operation and improved security measures, rather than closing boarder as a means of controlling terrorists.

Further, wolf is of the strong view that protectionist interest are also not as strong as they were historically and "the rise of the internationally integrated transnational company has reduced the ability and willingness of producers to wrap themselves in national flags". It is because "the concept of a purely national business sector has become, thankfully, increasingly irrelevant, diffusing protectionist lobbying." This apart, many people in high-income countries express concern about the decline in relative wages and opportunities for skilled labour, the political clout of these critics has, for better or worse, diminished with the general decline of the industrial working class. A web of strong international commitments also makes it far more difficult for protectionist interests of capture legislatures as they once did the final element of the 20th century collapse began with the rise of anti-liberal ideas. There are parallels today, particularly, in the groups united to protest global capitalism. But there are groups, which include environmentalists, development lobbies, populists, socialists and anarchists are "vastly less intellectually coherent than the opponents of liberalism of a century ago" wolf said. Further wolf concludes that they are united only in what they oppose and offer no alternative way of running an economy; hence a movement that offers only protest is unlikely to triumph.

Globalisation: Indian Approach

Globalisation is an issue that has been high on the research agenda for several years, spawning a vast and at times unwieldy literature. A concept often ill-defined, it has generated a plethora of unresolved and fiercely contested questions, the nature of which depends on which side of the ideological divide one stands.

Globalisation is a complex process that is having a massive impact on living standards across both the developed and developing world. It is helping to reduce poverty and raise living standards. However, it has deleterious consequences as well. For instance, it has been conclusively arrived at that in India, inter regional inequality appears to have widened during the globalization era. The challenge before India is in many ways unique. India is rich in knowledge and the production Technology and surprisingly this knowledge has not been reckoned as a commodity. It is only in the recent times this has changed somewhat, and India has rapidly increased its integration with the global economy. Indeed the World Bank recently judged India to be one of the worlds "fast globalizes". Since June 1991, India has been a member of a club of "globalizes".

Internationally, globalization has yielded impressive growth dividends, including for relatively poor countries. The list of 'post-1980 globalizes' includes Argentina, Brazil, china, Malaysia, Mexico, the Philippines and Thailand which, as a group, experienced an acceleration in average growth from 1.4 per cent per annum in the 1960's to 2.9 per cent per annum in the 1970's, 3.5 per cent in the 1980's and 5 per cent in the 1990's.

Since, India has steered its economic policies towards increased participation in the global economy, a range of political, ideological and economic parameters have been modified, while other are likely to be more drastically revised in the future. However, because of India's basic commitment to its constitution remains paramount, globalization will continue to be subject to the democratic process.

Globalisation and Indian Agriculture

Globalisation has profoundly affected both the ways of life and the livelihoods of indigenous people worldwide. Dr. D. Swaminathan, an Agricultural Scientist, deplores that one crore farmers in USA have been getting US$ 100 crore of subsidies per day as against 11 crore farmers in India who are desperately looking up to the skies without any substantial subsidy as in the case of their counterparts in the USA to adopt new technologies of production with the latest equipments, to buy improved seeds and pesticides to boost up their productivity levels. It is because of the fact the government of India under the dictates of World Bank has reduced significantly agriculture subdivides.

Globalisation of agriculture mainly implies the exposure of Indian agriculture to international market forces through free exports and imports of agricultural commodities. As a matter of fact, that government of India has already committed for the globalisation of Indian Economy. Globalisation of Indian agriculture, on the one hand, will provide it with opportunities to share the international market and on the other, will expose it to competition form foreign supplier in the domestic market and force the domestic production to adopt more efficient techniques of production. In general the economists hold that on the whole, India is likely to benefit form the globalisation of Indian agriculture. This is because India has a comparative cost advantage in the production of agricultural commodities. It is felt that agricultural exports form India are likely to increase significantly if the government follows policy of globalizing the Indian economy.

However, the immediate impact rise in agricultural exports will be an increase in the prices of agricultural commodities in the national market. And if these commodities include wheat and rice or other cereals, the vulnerable section of the society will be hit hard. This will necessitate a more effective implementation of the Public Distribution System (PDS). This may also result in food subsidies. One important way is to develop and adopt cost effective technology for production of agricultural products. Reduction in cost of production will surely keep the internal prices of agricultural commodities stable even when these are exported. National Agricultural Research System (NARS) needs to be revamped to suit the changing conditions in the country.

There exists a large potential for increasing exports of quite a few agricultural commodities produced in India. However, despite the great potential for increase in agricultural exports, various economists suggest caution in completely freeing exports, especially of food grains to other countries. There is a need to regulate the exports, not only for reason of food security but also for some other politico-economic considerations. Specific steps have to be earnestly taken to generate this surplus. This implies development of infrastructure especially irrigation and power research, extension of new technology to uncovered crops and areas, development of market infrastructure and a more efficient use of existing resources. Further, in view of the increasing competition in the world market, it will also be necessary to pay special attention to the improvement in the quality of the products to be exported. Import of agricultural commodities unrelated to the scarcity of these commodities in the country will only mean a wasteful use of foreign exchange.

Another reason for overseeing the imports of agricultural commodities is the need to ensure that the imported agricultural commodities are not hoarded for profiteering by the private individuals. Besides development of infrastructure, multinational can be allowed to develop agro-processing industries. But we have to be very cautions while recommending such a step for some other productive activities allied to agriculture. In this connection, we must refer to the consequences of having allowed them the right of fishing in the Indians seas. A large number of Indian fisherman has been rendered unemployed because of the grant of these rights to multinationals. However, the provisions of the TRIPS are likely to attract the development of agriculture rather adversely at least for some time. This provision implies the technologies used in the production to traded goods will be patented and their use for production will not be made by any country except the one where it has been patented. So far as agriculture is concerned, it is the cost of new varieties of imported seeds which will increase as the technology used in their development is obviously a foreign one. In order to overcome this problem, we have set up our own research projects to develop new seeds with indigenous technology.

India's agricultural scenario is lagging behind is substantiated with the following facts:

- India has 60 million hectares under irrigation comparative just 47 million in China and yet our food production only 22 million tones. Where as China products two and half times as much.
- In India, fruits and vegetables too, our position is as dismal with 9.7 per cent share of production in the farmer and 11 per cent share in the latter; we tragically processes less than 1 pr cent of our total production commercially. In contrast, Brazil processes 70 per cent of its fruits and vegetable production, Malaysia 83 per cent and Philippines 78 per cent.
- Intelligent application of new technologies called for immediately for new patterns of development in India to compete with other countries of the world.

The exact amount of foreign exchange earned through export of some specific variety of fruits grown in some pockets of Andhra Pradesh could not be presented here due to lack documented data. It is because of globalisation fruits grown in Anantapur district such as oranges, grapes, and promogantes could find markets in foreign countries. Similarly, grapes of Hyderabad and nearby places and mangoes of Guntur, Vijayawada and Rajamundry have been exported to markets of foreign countries. It was all made possible due to the fact that India is a member of club of globalisers and the latest technology-improved methods of preservation and new system of package methods. It is reported that such of those farmers who engaged in these trades could get good returns.

Five years after the WTO came into existence, the anticipated gains from the trade liberalization process in agriculture are partially non-existent. Since 1996-97, total agricultural exports have declined from US$ 6,828 million (Rs. 31,818 crore) to US$ 5,47 million (Rs. 25,513 crore) and agricultural imports have increased from US$ 39,132 million (Rs. 1,82,355 crore) to US$ 47,212 million (Rs. 2,20,008 crore). India exports a very small percentage of its production.

Globalisation is changing the structure of our agriculture. With almost 70 per cent Indians still are living on agriculture as against 5 per cent in the advanced countries. But it has been recorded that there has been a significant variations in the productive levels. The hectare-wise production of wheat, rice, cotton and peanuts in India is about 1/3rd of its western and even chine's counter part. To make things worse the Indian consumer may soon wooed over by cheaper foreign provisions like oil, rice and sugar.

Agriculture which is the backbone of our economy is already in the throes of crisis today. The costs of agriculture have gone up due to rise in the prices of seeds, fertilizers, water, and electricity and of course, labour whereas the prices of agricultural products have gone down. As a result farmers are unable to get even the cost prices. What is more regrettable is that farmers are not getting sufficient purchasers of their produces in man dies and they are unable to sell their harvests. The fact is that under the terms of WTO agreements on agriculture member countries have to import foreign goods in certain percentage even if the country is suffering over-production or/and farm prices are very low. These important items are mainly food grains, fertilizers, edible oils, drugs and synthetic yarns.

In per capita availability of agricultural land India is low and the number of agriculture holdings of less than a hectare has been on the rise. Under this situation globalisation is likely to throw our agriculture into deep crisis. The globalisation process has started casting its gloomy shadows on our agriculture and through that over the entire economy.

References

Francis Cherumilam: Business and Government, Himalaya Publishing House, Bangalore, 2003.

Gursharan Singh Kainth (Ed.): Export potential of Indian Agriculture, regency Publications, New Delhi, 2002.

Jonathan Michie (Ed): The handbook of Globalisation, University of London, 2003.

Rameshchandra: LPG and Indian Economy, Isha Books, Delhi, 2004.

3

Globalisation and Dalits

The world witnessed economic reforms, nay, and economic liberalism since the last quarter of the 20th century. The economic liberalism swept the old and the conservative protectionist strategies of the countries across the world, including both the Western and Eastern parts of the globe. Economic liberalism allowed free movement of not only goods, services and manpower but also capital across the world, making it convenient to manufacture and market goods and services with the available local resources of both manpower and physical resources. The phenomenon explained above may be addressed as the process of globalisation. The Central theme of the globalisation is to achieve global welfare through the utilization of local resources, which are found abundant in various parts of the globe?

Globalisation, by way of erasing national boundaries, treated the world as a single habitat-global village. Each country in the global village has been trying to capture and share world market to the extent possible by way of increasing productivity levels of the goods in which they enjoy relative disadvantage regardless of fast depletion of the scarce natural resources, some of which may be non-renewable and lost for ever once used.

Each country has been trying to steal a march over the other countries. In the rat-race of capturing global market. In the process, the already developed countries reap all the benefits of globalisation adopting scale of economies technologies in production and thus by extending markets to sell their products at the most competitive prices through their MNC's; this effectively checks the entry of new producers in the countries concerned making it further difficult to progress industrially. As a consequence of this trend, most of the developing countries in respect of industrial progress not only pushed back but also resulted in the closure of many industrial units engaged in manufacture of the MNC's goods.

The Indian Industrial sector has tasted this bitter experience which has resulted in closure of many traditional, (village and cottage industries) and modern industries too resulted in increasing the number of army of industrial unemployees in the country.

Globalisation implies opening up the economy to the private sector, by sale of whole or part of Government owned equity in nationalized industries or other commercial enterprises to private sector or allowing private sector to operate in fields earlier reserved for the Government sector.

Globalisation implies integrating to the economy of a country with the world economy. In the Indian context it implies relaxation of restrictions on participation of foreign direct investment, multinational corporations and foreign collaborations, and liberalization of imports and exports. The thrust to globalisation has been provided since the announcement of new industrial and trade policies of India in July 1991.

Dr. B.R. Ambedkar's Concern for Dalits

Dr. B. R. Ambedkar advocated several policies and strategies to liberate that 'Dalits' from deprivation, poverty and social stigma to development and social reorganization. He devoted considerable attention to analyze the economic, social and political dimensions of poverty of Dalits with historical evidences within a frame work i.e. basically a legal system in a democratic set up. His legacy to the Dalits is primarily the constitutional safeguards for the scheduled castes. As a means for liberating and enabling their deliverance from deprivation and social stigma.

Dalits meaning 'broken' and oppresses' is synonymous for the 'Depressed Classes' (D.C's). To a great extent both these terms are now too freely and indiscriminately applied to an assortment of social groups, recently labeled as depressed, deprived, disabled, disadvantaged, downtrodden, weaker sections, other backward castes (OBC's), minorities, Scheduled Tribes

(ST's) untouchables (SC's), Harijans and others. Ambedkar several times expressed his dissatisfaction at lumping all those groups and using the terms DC's and Dalits to include all categories. He expected to equip them with political power to improve their socio-economic, educational and cultural conditions, in an attempt to actualize their gradual deliverance from deprivation to development from social stigma to social respect, and social equality.

The Dalits thus refers to SC and ST communities together privatization has been accepted and implemented as one of the instruments of economic reforms in India which are aimed not only to overcome economic crisis but to take economy on the fast track of development. In an effort to achieve this goal the Government of India has allowed the private industrialists or private industrialists with the partnership of foreign private parties to start all types of industries in the public sector owing to their strategic importance in safeguarding the nation both from within and outside forces.

Definition of the Word 'Dalit'

The category of the people Dalit was defined by the different social scientists in different ways. For Gail Omvedt the 'Dalit Movement' is akin to Marxist theorist Immanuel Wallerstein's 'anti-systemic movements'. Gail Omvedt says that "This kind of movement challenged and sought to transform the basic structure of the Indian social system, replacing caste and the accompanying social oppression, economic exploitation and political domination by an egalitarian society".

Further, she argues that any revolutionary movement has to have emancipator and broad democratic ideology with values of freedom, equality and autonomy as it general framework. Thus, in this sense the Dalit Movement for Gail Omvedt is more 'nationalistic' than the elite controlled National Movement. Gail Omvedt's basic reference points are Marxism in identifying the 'dalit' category. According to Gopal Guru there were two interpretations of the term 'Dalit'. According to him the non-dalit writers tend to differ radically from the dalit writers in the interpretation of the term 'Dalit'. While the non-dalit tend to patronize the Dalits by calling them, as Gandhiji termed 'Harijan' or as 'Asprushta' used by the Maharastrian Brahmin reformer, S.M. Mate. The non-dalit writers identify themselves in various terms as 'Dalit', 'ex-untouchables', 'Adidravidas', 'Adikarnataka', 'Adihindu', or the more recent 'Dalitbahujan' propagated by Kansi Ram's political party, Bahujan Samajvad Party.

For Kansi Ram, however, 'dalitbahujan' includes not only the untouchables or the Scheduled Caste but also Scheduled Tribes and Other Backward Castes. The noted dalit writer of Andhra Pradesh. Kancha Illaih also endorses the definition of Kansiram's term 'Dalitbahujan'. In his book 'why I am not Hindu', he rejects Mahatma Phule's term 'Shudra' or 'Atishudra' as the term 'Shudra' is given by the upper class and was used in a derogatory sense. For Illaih it does not communicate a feeling of self-respect and political assertion. Moreover, according to Illaih the term Shudra does not include the Dalits as they were outside the purview of Hinduism. For him, the term 'dalit' refers only to the oppressed class, the untouchables. For Illaih the word 'bahujan' before 'dalit' is desirable as it means 'majority' and includes not only the 'Dalits' but also the OBCs.

However, Illaih does not want to include the STs in this category because they do not belong to the Hindu caste system. Thus, Illaih contradicts himself by arguing that the dalitbahujan do not belong to the Hindu caste order and at the same time rejects the inclusion of the STs in the 'dalitbahujan' fold. To sum up, for Kancha illaih 'dalitbahujan' are "the people and castes that form the exploited and suppressed majority" But, another noted dalit writer Gopal Guru does not endorse to kansiram and Kancha Illaih's term 'dalitbahujan'. For Guru 'dalitbahujan' leaders follow 'empty emotionalism' in rejecting the term 'Harijans' and in including the various categories like the STs and the OBCs. Guru accepts the term 'dalit' and not 'bahujan' with it for two reasons. Guru says that by bringing in the term 'bahujan' the 'historicity of the word 'dalit' is negated as the 'Dalitbahujan' term brings in mere statistical and computer entity for the manipulation by the power hungry political parties and the term 'Dalit' without the tag 'bahujan' is not "available for the chicanery of political manipulation or calculation whether external or internal".

Gopal Guru further argues that the term 'Dalit' forms a kind of multiple identities as the category 'Dalit' constitutes oppressed people from all over the continent of India who have their distinct regional identities as well. He contrasts between what he calls 'superficial consciousness' and deep consciousness' of the oppressed category. The term 'Dalit' has to permeate among various levels of multiple identities of the oppressed people. Gopal Guru suggests the plurality that exists among the 'Dalits' and the need to transcend these levels to form a common identity for the purpose of creating a society, which is free from coercion and exploitation. For P.S. Krishna the term 'dalit' is an expression of their self-assertion as against the manes imposed by the upper castes such as 'chandala' or 'dhed'. P.S. Krishna gives another dimension to the term 'dalit' by expanding as 'Vidrohi-Dalit' which means the Oppressed Revolt. He includes the STs and the OBC's in the fray and calls them 'sah-dalit' meaning co-oppressed, 'Vishal-Dalit' meaning the oppressed in the wider sense of the term respectively.

For P.S. Krishna it is with the help of all these categories of Dalits a peaceful, democratic mass movement could to be conducted for the assertion of identity of the Dalits. While the 'dalit' scholars and the non-dalit scholars in general accepted the term 'dalit' as the desired term the British Government and the Government of India studiously avoided all the above terms and opted for more neutral term, as the 'Depressed classes', or the most recent term, as 'Scheduled Castes/Tribes'. Dr. Ambedkar too used the terms like 'Depressed Classes', 'Scheduled castes', 'Bahishkrit' and 'Pad Dalit' as the occasion demanded. The other western scholars like Harold Isaac, Barbara Joshi and Lelah Dushkin called them as ex-untouchables, exterior castes or in touchable castes. Eleanor Zelliot and Gail Omvedt refer to them as 'dalit'.

Dr. Ambedkar defined 'dalit' or 'dalithood' as 'a kind of life condition that characterizes the exploitation, suppression and marginalization of dalit people by the social, economic, cultural and political domination of the upper castes' Brahminical ideology. One movement, which used the term 'dalit' extensively, was the dalit Panthers of Maharastra. According to the Dalit Panthers the term Dalit "is a revolutionary one for its hermeneutic ability to recover the revolutionary meaning of the historical past of the Dalit people". But the Dalit Panthers included other categories of he oppressed namely, the tribals, toiling classes and women thus making the concept of 'Dalit' more broader in its perception.

Thus, various scholars define the category 'dalit' in almost the same way, as the category of people who have been oppressed in the name of religion, who have been silenced for centuries by the Hindu caste order. The term 'Dalit' is very important for this category of people as it gives a distinct identity of their own. Their oppressions do not impose it on them. Even though, there is general agreement in the term 'Dalit' as the identity of the oppressed, there is a lot of argument as to who constitute this category called 'Dalit'. Most of the scholars starting from mahatma Phule, Dr. Ambedkar, Periyar, to the present like Kancha Illiah, Kanshi Ram, the Dalit Christian writers like John Massey, Walter Fernandez, and so on have include all the oppressed into the fold of the category 'Dalit' irrespective of the religion, caste, tribe or gender. However, recent dalit writer like Gopal Guru wants to stay away with the state constituted categories like Scheduled Castes/Tribes, and Other Backward Castes as according to Gopal Guru it is deliberate and artificially constructed. And also these state constructed terms work as charity rather than on equal terms.

Economic Reforms, Globalisation and Dalits

Economic Reforms in India were introduced in 1991 with

near unanimity among major political parties. The new Economic, reforms were aimed to accelerate the process of the development in India. The government of India decided to implement new economic reforms with the major policy prescription of privatization and globalisation (LPG). The article attempts to assess the impact of globalisation on the status of Dalits in the country.

Money and Markets are the Gods of Globalisation. Globalisation is a movement of large scale transfer of capital from developed countries to all over the world for their selfish and sustained development. Siglitz exposes the hypocrisy of Western countries: "The Western countries have pushed poor countries to eliminate trade barriers, but kept up their own barriers, preventing developing countries from exporting their agricultural products and so depriving them; of desperately needed export income.

The proponents of globalization have been propagating a minimal role for the state accompanied with a maximum role for the markets and welfare aspects of socially and economically weaker sections-Dalits, did not get the needed support in most of the developing countries like India. But there is an increasing trend towards erosion of sovereignty of nation-states. Pressure of multi-national corporations (MNCs), the IMF and World Bank force governments to take decisions about privatization of public enterprises, opening of FDI in several sectors, such as retail trade, consumer goods like potato chips, hurting small and medium enterprises, leading to their closure and resultant unemployment. Globalizations have also resulted in widening inequalities between the forward and backward states in India and also within groups have helped to create an elite. As a consequence, exclusion of marginalized groups, the poor and the asset less is taking place. It has also led to declining earnings of unskilled labour, destruction of environment and deprivation of basic human rights including the right to work and rights at work place. Globalization has led to more insecurity for workers, increased militancy of employers against workers and enhanced the phenomenon of lock-outs.

Moreover, markets have failed to provide resources for the development of infrastructure, more especially in rural areas where a majority of Dalits live. Globalization has bypassed agriculture the principal source of livelihood of over 60 percent of the population. Moreover, globalization triggered the process of privatization; but the entry of powerful MNCs replaced public monopolies with private monopolies. "Whether the privatized monopolies were more efficient in production than government, they were often more efficient in exploiting their monopoly position; consumers suffered as a result."

It is now well recognized that globalization lacks social responsibility of taking care of the welfare of the Dalits. But to restore more social responsibility and the need to create conditions for decent work and a 'decent society' which cares for the poor, the weaker sections, the small entrepreneur, it is vitally necessary to strengthen the regulatory and promotional role of the state. The present situation in which 'government reigns, but global capital rules' has to be altered in a fundamental sense. D. Narasimha Reddy in his presidential address to the India Society of Labour Economics (2004) concluded: "That markets have a place but the task is to place the markets in their place. Markets should not be allowed to destroy the social fabric, which even the state cannot reconstruct easily. Markets need to be regulated in order to prevent them from causing social disruption. The task of ensuring 'decent work' in the third world is a task or restoring the state its rightful place in development".

The ILO Report recording the perception of globalization mentions: "In India, the message was more mixed; there had been winners and losers. The lives of the educated and the rich had been enriched by globalization. The information technology (IT) sector was a particular beneficiary. But the benefits had not yet reached the majority, which includes Dalits and new risks had cropped up for the losers-the socially deprived and rural poor. Significant numbers of 'non-perennial' poor, who had worked hard to escape poverty, were finding their gains reversed....power was shifting from elected local institutions to unaccountable transnational bodies." Obviously, such a perception of globalization is not in the interest of the Dalits.

Impact of Globalisation on Dalits in India

It is reported that it was only the rich upper class people who have purchased Government equities the public sectors, where the process of disinvestment was undertaken in the recent past. It is rather strange to notice that neither OBC's nor the Dalits have purchased the equities of the public sectors. That is to say that the Dalits and the OBC's could not become the owners in of the industries where disinvestments operation was conducted during the reforms period.

A large number of industrial units have come up in the country in the private sector after July 24, 1991. Where the recruitment of required manpower carried out without following the rule of reservation; this has seriously restricted the participation of Dalits in the in production sector of India and thus deprived of them from getting sustained stream of income generating jobs to improve their socio-economic conditions.

It took more than 20 years to reach the institutional privilege/benefits to the Dalits in India. The VI Five Year Plan formulated for the first time with a special component plan to enable half of SC's families to cross over the poverty line within a short period. This shows the shift of emphasis from welfare to family beneficiary oriented schemes within the general frame work of socio-economic programmes specially designed and directed for the benefits of the Dalits. The same trend continued even during the VII plan also. The plight of the Dalits under new economic reforms-privatization and globalisation explained is in the following paragraphs.

The VIII Five Year Plan launched with the component economic reforms of LPG. Since, the private sector was allowed to operate large scale, corporate culture began to acquire commanding heights. The country witnessed fast growth of professional and other new educational institutions where the organizers of these institutions ensure to provide quality education that helps to get placement in companies both within and outside country with high salaries.

Here it should be mentioned that entry or admission into these institutions is not open to all. On the other hand, the entry is restricted to such of those students who can pay high fees and other payments to the managements and Dalits being poor could not find entry into these institutions; they can hope to educate their children in the government institutions where the rule of reservation is being practised. And the corporate institutions, certainly, have an edge over the Government run institutions, in respect of in passing quality education as they do not face resources constraint of any sort. Thus it clearly states that a vast majority of Dalits do not have access to quality education as they do not have the required where-withal to admit their children in the corporate sector institutions.

Dropout Rates

The Era of Economic Reforms witnessed a large scale mechanization of agriculture in the country. Tracterisation has been on its increasing operation; 4 or 5 tractors taking care of all the agricultural operations in a relative's big village as such this trend fast replaced Dalits who are hitherto engaged in agricultural operations were force to migrate to urban centres finding themselves as loaders and un-loaders of weights in the shopping malls, Bus stations and Railway stations. Women too, lost traditional occupations in agricultural sector as more and more labour saving devises such as harvesters and crop cutters (crop tigers) increasingly used in the agricultural sector. Along with men and women also migrated to urban centres and employed themselves as domestic servants and in other menial services. The situation uprooted Dalits from their traditional habitats and thus made them to migrate in search of alternative livelihoods in urban centres which are already over burden with socio-economic overheads consequent on worsening conditions in slum areas or mushroom growth of new slum dwellings in and around metropolis.

With regard to educational aspects the status of Dalits is very poor; in the sense that the drop-out rates are very high; the drop-out rate is in the range of 45 per cent to 60 per cent in the Primary and Middle Schools levels itself making it all the more difficult to fill up reservation quota in the higher educational institutions even after allowing elimination of Creamy Layer as per the Supreme Court verdict. This is largely due to conspicuous absence of sustained income levels of the Dalits during the economic reform period.

This fact is further reinforced by the Supreme Court's recent judgment: The Supreme Court's recent verdict-'No quota in unaided private colleges'-came as a rude shock to the Dalits and other Backward Communities (OBC's). The Supreme Court on 12/08/2005, Friday held that unaided minority and non-minority institutions had absolute rights to admit students of their choice in Medicine, Engineering and other professional courses without Government interference.

A seven-judge Constitution Bench has abolished the State quota and reservation in unaided, private minority and non-minority colleges. The judgment would be effective from the next academic year, 2006-07.

M. R. Justice Lahoti writing the unanimous judgment, said, "Merely because the resources of the State in providing professional education are limited, private educational institutions, which intend to provide better professional education, cannot be forced by the state to make admissions available on the basis of (the) reservation policy to less meritorious candidates". (The Hindu, August 13, 2005, Saturday, Banglore Edition)

As a result of this, the Dalits are deprived of quality education and employment opportunity in high profile institutions as the corporate sector is not implementing constitutional provisions for the Dalits.

Although the content of the globalisation openly declares hat the local or the national resources would be used to heighten the global welfare do not speak in favour of the most of the developing countries, like India. For instance, such of those Dalits who were engaged in manufacture and to marketing of foot-wear have to given up there up profession, for they could not be face competition of the international organizations which have advance infrastructural facilities both to manufacture and to marketing a variety of foot-wear across the globe, selling at highly competitive prices. Dalits being poor who use to work with traditional skills produce foot-wear and marketed them in their local areas/sandies are totally vanished from the scene because of the globalisation phenomenon.

From the early 1990's the farmers in India have been enjoying freedom in selection of methods in the process of agricultural production; there were allowed to use all kinds of technologies to modernize their agriculture so as to meet the challenges at the global level. In order to save labour, interlaid, the farmers took to rapid mechanization of agriculture, with the use of tractors, threshers, harvesters, crop-tiger and power-driven-sprayers. The skilled and trained labour found jobs leaving behind the unskilled and untrained Dalits without a gainful employment in rural areas and the situation forced them to migrate to cities in search of some job for their survival. This has shattered their families and left them to lead a life in more miserable conditions. The survey that was conducted in Anantapur District revealed the fact that the number of households that belonged of SC's and ST's have increase, significantly in Anantapur city after 1995 onwards; and most of them live in unhygienic slum conditions.

Conclusion

One finds there exists an uneven distribution of wealth in India; nearly, 80 per cent of the wealth owned by the top 20 per cent of the population while 80 per cent of the population command only 20 per cent of the wealth in India. The present Economic Reforms implemented, has allowed the rich become richer and the poor not becoming better. The Dalits and the OBC's covered under the category of the 80 per cent of the people commanding 20 per cent of the wealth in the country do not seemed to have improved their Socio-Economic status under reforms period. Hence, it is imperative to review the existing social security measures intended for the Dalits and OBC's in the country.

The Economic Reforms, (LPG) instead of improving Dalits and OBC's Socio-Economic status should not allow them to slip down from the existing position. Infact, the relative position of the Dalits worsened as other sections of the society have stolen a march over the Dalits who are mostly landless, shelterless caught in debt trap, and living below the poverty line. As already point out, globalisation enriched the educated and propertied sections of the society, high drop-out rate of Dalits students of primary and middle levels came in the way of their socio-economic development. Since the education is the prime factor of socio-economic transformation/improvement recognizing this, the governments have to review and redraft the policy prescriptions so as to provide the needed social-security measures for the upliftment of Dalits under globalisation, which has fast picked up its momentum in the recent times.

4

Human Resource Concerns under Globalisation

Introduction

Triggered by globalisation, most of the countries in the world have been trying to capture the World market through their competitive spirit, trying to excel its neighbouring countries in an attempt to achieve economic prosperity by way of optimal utilization of all its resources-both human and physical. Globalisation has brought far reaching changes at the global level. Former enemies had turned friends in the Post-Cold War new age of globalisation. The only interest that mattered now is business-money and markets. The 21st century has been referred by many as one of interdependence of nations, leading to massive economic activity. Globalisation had integrated economies and created a new global economic architecture unheard of in the last century. Globalisation thus refers to geographical shifts in domestic economic activity around the World and away from nation-states. It is rather painful to state the unskilled workers, who are in large number, will be hard hit by the globalisation. However, proponents of international trade, based on their experience, suggest under globalisation all nations will gain in the long run.

The debate on merits of globalisation continues, with one side argument that it raises living standards and the others that it worsens poverty and inequality. Certainly, economic globalisation has led to increased wealth for many in some countries. But it also led to shattering economic crisis, collapse in standard of living, widespread societal and ethnic conflict, social disintegration and greatly increased insecurity for disproportionately large part of the world's population. Martin Wolf, Associate Editor and Chief Economics Commentator, at the 'Financial Times' offered a robust defense of globalization and upbeat assessment of its prospects. In discussing his new book "why Globalisation Works" he has rebutted claims that globalization undermines sovereignty, weakens democracy, intensifies inequality, favours 'exploitative' multinational corporations, and devastates the environment.

Martin Wolf has conceded that China and India – opponents of economic integration could yet do grave damage. However, he strongly feels that the forces against globalization are not strong enough to cause its (globalization) disintegration as it seemed implausible that global disintegration would collapse, as it had in the interwar years of the early 20th century as a consequence of international rivalries, economic instability, protectionist interests and anti-liberal ideas.

Martin wolf has advanced four fundamental strong grounds in defense to say why globalization works. They are:

1. There is for the moment, a single in disputed hegemony – the United States and war among great powers in the near future seems unlikely;
2. All the great powers seem to have abandoned the nation that property derives from the territorial gains and plunder rather than from internal economic development and peaceful exchange;
3. All the great powers now share a commitment to market-led economic development and international economic and political integration of some kind; and
4. Global institutions and close international cooperation reinforce the basic stability of the political order.

The breakdown of the early 20th century order occurred in large part because of the pressures to accommodate rising powers in the global economic and political order. "If the United States remain wedded to nations of global primacy rather than of a shared global order, conflict with a rising china would seem almost inevitable", wolf cautioned. In addition to these political pressures, China's ascent will force uncomfortable economic adjustment on the rest of the world-a phenomenon that is already fueling protectionist pressures in a number of countries. But a greater threat to the world's commitment to open boarders is mega terrorism.

Hence, wolf called for global co-operation and improved security measures, rather than closing boarder as a means of controlling terrorists.

Further, wolf is of the strong view that protectionist interest are also not as strong as they were historically and "the rise of the internationally integrated transnational company has reduced the ability and willingness of producers to wrap themselves in national flags". It is because "the concept of a purely national business sector has become, thankfully, increasingly irrelevant, diffusing protectionist lobbying". This apart, many people in high-income countries express concern about the decline in relative wages and opportunities for skilled labour, the political clout of these critics has, for better or worse, diminished with the general decline of the industrial working class. A web of strong international commitments also makes it far more difficult for protectionist interests of capture legislatures as they once did the final element of the 20th century collapse began with the rise of anti-liberal ideas. There are parallels today, particularly, in the groups united to protest global capitalism. But there are groups, which include environmentalists, development lobbies, populists, socialists and anarchists are "vastly less intellectually coherent than the opponents of liberalism of a century ago" wolf said. Further wolf concludes that they are united only in what they oppose and offer no alternative way of running an economy; hence a movement that offers only protest is unlikely to triumph.

Globalisation is an issue that has been high on the research agenda for several years, spawning a vast and at times unwieldy literature. A concept often ill-defined, it has generated a plethora of unresolved and fiercely contested questions, the nature of which depends on which side of the ideological divide one stands.

Globalisation is a complex process that is having a massive impact on living standards across both the developed and developing world. It is helping to reduce poverty and raise living standards. However, it has deleterious consequences as well. For instance, it has been conclusively arrived at that in India, inter regional inequality appears to have widened during the globalization era. The challenge before India is in many ways unique. India is rich in knowledge and the production Technology and surprisingly this knowledge has not been reckoned as a commodity. It is only in the recent times this has changed somewhat, and India has rapidly increased its integration with the global economy. Indeed the World Bank recently judged India to be one of the worlds "fast globalizes". Since June 1991, India has been a member of a club of "globalizes".

Internationally, globalization has yielded impressive growth dividends, including for relatively poor countries. The list of 'post-1980 globalizes' includes Argentina, Brazil, china, Malaysia, Mexico, the Philippines and Thailand which, as a group, experienced an acceleration in average growth from 1.4 per cent per annum in the 1960's to 2.9 per cent per annum in the 1970's, 3.5 per cent in the 1980's and 5 per cent in the 1990's.

Since, India has steered its economic policies towards increased participation in the global economy, a range of political, ideological and economic parameters have been modified, while other are likely to be more drastically revised in the future. However, because of India's basic commitment to its constitution remains paramount, globalization will continue to be subject to the democratic process.

India has experienced urban-rural divide during globalisation Indian cities are booming the country-side is suffering as a result of global phenomenon. The situation poses a challenge being to ensure economic prosperity to all in the country through optimum utilization of resources. An attempt is made here as how the challenges of globalisation met through Human Resource Development in Andhra Pradesh, with reference to Andhra Pradesh State Council for Higher Education (APSCHE).

Meeting the Challenges of HRD under Globalisation

As on today, the number of Universities in India is 350; of which 25, including Deemed Universities, are in Andhra Pradesh.

That means the state accounts for slightly over 7 per cent of the total number of Universities in the country. The number of Universities in the state was only 3 in 1956 which rose to 4 in 1970 and by 2007 their increased to 25 during the academic year 2006-07, which clearly states educational advancement stated picking up rather fast from 1990 onwards. It's worth recording that the impressive role played the APSCHE in the field of Higher Education in the state.

Facts presented in Table 4.1 explain Higher Educational opportunities created by the APSCHE over a period of 6 years, from 2001 to 2007. The private sector in the state found that it as a good opportunity to invest in the Higher Education as it ensured quick and lucrative returns on their investment. A cursory glance at the table mirrors this trend and the private sector made a quantum jump in providing Higher Education in the state as per the regulations of the APSCHE.

Engineering Colleges: The A.P. state had only 27 Engineering Colleges both under the government and private sectors by 1990; they rose to 105 in 2000-01 and further their number rose to 269 with an intake capacity 93,385 by 2006-07.

M.C.A. Colleges: The total number of colleges offering M.C.A. course was 168 with an intake of 6,440 while 2000-01; their number shot up to 381 within intake of 21,850 by 2006-07.

M.B.A Colleges: The total number of colleges offering M.B.A. in 2000 was 117 with an intake of 4,505 and their number rose to 278 with an intake of 16,875 during the year 2006-07.

Pharmacy Colleges: The total number of Pharmacy Colleges during the year 2006-07 was 103 with a take capacity of 6,080 as against 60 and 4,800 respectively for the year 2000-01.

Colleges offering B.Ed. Course: The total number of colleges offering B.Ed. Course in the state for the year 2006-07 was 345 with an intake of 38,829 as against 87 and 11,456 respectively for the year 2000-01.

Law Colleges: Unlike the other professional courses law course is lagging behind. That means the response by the private sector in this regard is rather poor. The fact is evidenced by the factual information presented in the Table 4.1. The total number of law colleges during the year 2000-01 was 42 with an intake of 9,760 which rose to 53 with an intake of 10,800 during the year 2006-07.

Table 4.1: Position of Higher Education during the Academic Years 2000-01 to 2006-07 in Andhra Pradesh

S. No	Course	2000-01		2006-07	
		No. of Colleges	Intake	No. of Colleges	Intake
I. Professional					
1.	Engineering	105	80,125	269	93,385
2.	M.C.A.	168	6,440	381	21,850
3.	M.B.A.	117	4,505	278	16,875
4.	Pharmacy	60	4,800	103	6,080
5.	B.Ed.	87	11,456	345	38,829
6.	Law	42	9,760	53	10,800
Total		579	1,17,086	1,429	1,87,819
II. Non-Professional					
1.	General Degree (B.A., B.Sc., B.Com. and B.Com. Computers)	989	2,87,427	1,670	4,25,811
2.	PG Courses	196	22,146	280	30,600
Total		1,185	3,09,573	1,950	4,56,411

Source: Andhra Pradesh State Council for Higher Education, Hyderabad.

General Degree Courses: The Colleges offering courses, such as, traditional B.A., B.Sc., B.Com. and B.Com. Computers are referred as general degree courses. There were 989 degree colleges with an intake of 2,87,427 for the year 2000-01; and their size shot up to 1,670 with an intake of 4,25,811 during the year

2006-07. It is significant to state that here that more than 80 per cent of these colleges are being owned by private managements.

PG Courses: The total number of colleges offering PG Courses was 196 with an intake of 22,146 during the year 2000-01 and their number increased to 280 with an intake of 30,600 during the year 2006-07.

Globalisation: Tilt towards Professional Courses

In order to seize the opportunity of getting quick returns under globalization, the private investors came forward to establish professional colleges in the state. The public have also sustained the interest of the private investors by way of admitting their wards into various professional courses especially computer and business oriented courses which offered lot of job potential both at the National and the Global levels. As a result the state has witnessed an abnormal growth (excluding Medical, Polytechnic, Agriculture, and Veterinary Courses) of professional colleges. The professional courses recorded an increase of nearly 247 per cent while the non professional colleges increased by about 165 per cent. In the case of enrolment of students the professional colleges accounted for 160 per cent while non-professional colleges 147 per cent during the period 2000-01 to 2006-07. Thus, based on the above analysis one can infer that the public have been showing sustained response to such of those courses which meet the job requirement under globalization.

Poor Quality of Human Resource Development

It is rather painful to state that only 15 per cent of the Engineering graduates who passed out in the state colleges in the possessed competence, befitting to their degrees. That means, the majority of engineering colleges have not been equipped with competent teaching faculty, libraries with up to date publications and necessary laboratory facilities. This is a serious lapse which is causing a lot of concern in the state.

The fate of non-professional colleges is far too worse. The student strength in a science section is 90; and student strength in Arts section is 150 in most of the Government colleges in the state. The ratio of teacher-students is unmanageable and as such teacher can hardly monitor the student's progress either in the class or in the laboratory. Added to this, most of the private colleges are ill-equipped in respect of competent staff, library and laboratory and in other aspects. Non-professional students whose strength is 4,56,411 are reeling under uncertainty situation without any hope to get placement to eke-out their livelihoods. The situation calls for positive response from the concerned to create enough of job opportunities to the non-professional graduates who are more in number compared to all the professional graduates put together in the state

APSCHE's Role in Promotion of HRD in Andhra Pradesh

Of late, the Andhra Pradesh State Council for Higher Education (APSCHE) has been playing pivotal role in creation of APSCHE better opportunities in respect of Human Resource Development (HRD). The APSCHE has been providing congenial atmosphere in the state to promote higher education in the private sector. The APSCHE has been properly monitoring the whole process of HRD in the state.

To seize the job opportunities in Software sector, soft-skills have been up-grade through the establish of language laps in the Degree Colleges across the state.

The APSCHE initiated a new approach where by placement for the professionals made easy through campus selections, thousands of professionals such as- B. Tech's, M.C.A's, M.B.A's found good placements in many Soft-Ware and MNCs within and outside the country.

The another novel project launched by the APSCHE is that of Academy-Industry interaction to bring in appropriate changes/ modifications/omissions and commissions in the existing syllabai in such a way as to met require the requirements of the industry. Through this process the APSCHE has aimed to meet the job requirement of non-professional graduates in the state.

The APSCHE has made efforts to launch this programme to come into effect from the academic year 2006-07. Under this scheme one more new paper annually added to the existing syllabai and thus preparing non-professional graduates to have an easy entry into the job market. For instance B.Com graduates will be trained in the course of insurance and B.Sc. (B.Zc.) students would be trained in Medical Transcription course. The courses of this type certainly equip them with the necessary skills as required by the industry and thus help them to find jobs across the globe.

Conclusion

Under globalisation the rich have access to both knowledge and career as the corporate sector extends all the services to monied people. The poor who cannot find entry into corporate schools/colleges are denied of access to both knowledge and career. As such the yawning gulf between the rich and poor is ever widening under globalisation.

In order to meet the challenges of Human Resource Development (HRD) under globalisation the Andhra Pradesh State Council for Higher Education (APSCHE) has a responsibility to tone-up quality of education both in the professional and non-professional colleges in the state. It cannot feel smug just by sanctioning courses but all efforts should be made to monitor and regulate the courses sanctioned to endow the youth with necessary knowledge and skills to enable them to find a placement to fetches them reasonable income which help them to improve their quality of life.

References

Frans. J. Schuurman, (2000), "Globalisation and Development Studies", Sage Publications, New Delhi.

Gurshran Singh Kainth (Ed), (2002), "Export Potential of Indian Agriculture", Regency Publications, New Delhi.

Jonathan Michie (Ed), (2003), "The Handbook of Globalisation", University of London.

Mol. Arthur, P.J. (2001), "Globalisation and Environmental Reforms", Cambridge, Mass. M.I.T.

Ramesh Chandra, (2004), "LPG and Indian Economy", Isha Books, Delhi-110033.

5

Plight of Dalits under Privatisation and Globalisation

Economic Reforms, Privatisation and Globalisation

Economic Reforms in India were introduced in 1991 with near unanimity among major political parties in recent of their introduction and implementation. The new Economic, reforms were aimed to accelerate the process of the development in India. The government of India decided to implement new economic reforms with the major policy prescription of privatization and globalisation. The article attempts to assess the impact of privatization and globalisation on the state of Dalits in the country.

Privatization implies opening up the economy to the private sector, by sale of whole or part of Government owned equity in nationalized industries or other commercial enterprises to private sector or allowing private sector to operate in fields earlier reserved for the Government sector.

Globalisation implies integrating to the economy of a country with the world economy. In the Indian context it implies relaxation of restrictions on participation of foreign direct investment, multinational corporations and foreign collaborations, and liberalization of imports and exports. The thrust to globalisation has been provided since the announcement of new industrial and trade policies of India in July 1991.

Dr. B.R. Ambedkar advocated several policies and strategies to liberate that 'Dalits' from deprivation, poverty and social stigma to development and social recognisation. He devoted considerable attention to analyse the economic, social and political dimensions of poverty of Dalits with historical evidences within a frame work i.e. basically a legal system in a democratic set up. His legacy to the Dalits is primarily the constitutional safeguards for the scheduled castes. As a means for liberating and enabling their deliverance from deprivation and social stigma.

Dalits meaning 'broken' and oppresses' is synonymous for the 'Depressed Classes' (D.C's). To a great extent both these terms are now too freely and indiscriminately applied to an assortment of social groups, recently labeled as depressed, deprived, disabled, disadvantaged, downtrodden, weaker sections, other backward castes (OBC's), minorities, Scheduled Tribes (ST's) untouchables (SC's), Harijans and others. Ambedkar several times expressed his dissatisfaction at lumping all those groups and using the terms DC's and Dalits to include all categories. He expected to equip them with political power to improve their socio-economic, educational and cultural conditions, in an attempt to actualize their gradual deliverance from deprivation to development from social stigma to social respect, and social equality.

The Dalits, thus refers to SC and ST communities together privatization has been accepted and implemented as one of the instruments of economic reforms in India which are aimed not only to over come economic crisis but to take economy on the fast track of development. In an effort to achieve this goal the Government of India has allowed the private industrialists or private industrialists with the partnership of foreign private parties to start all types of industries in the public sector owing to their strategic importance in safeguarding the nation both from within and outside forces.

Impact of Economic Reforms on Dalits in India

It is reported that it was only the rich upper class people who have purchased Government equities the public sectors, where the process of disinvestment was undertaken in the recent past. It is rather strange to notice that neither OBC's nor the Dalits have purchased the equities of the public sectors. That is to say that the Dalits and the OBC's could not become the owners in of the industries where disinvestments operation was conducted during the reforms period.

A large number of industrial units have come up in the country in the private sector after July 24, 1991. Where the recruitment of required manpower executed without following the reservation; this has seriously restricted the participation of Dalits in the in production sector of India and thus deprived of them from getting secured jobs to improve their economic conditions.

It took more than 20 years to reach the institutional privilege/benefits to the Dalits in India. The VI Five Year Plan formulated for the first time with a special component plan to enable half of SC's families to cross over the poverty line within a short period. This shows the shift of emphasis from welfare to family beneficiary oriented schemes within the general frame work of socio-economic programmes specially designed and directed for the benefits of the Dalits. The same trend continued even during the VII plan also. The plight of the Dalits under new economic reforms-privatisation and globalisation explained is in the following paragraphs.

The VIII Five Year Plan launched with the component economic reforms of privatization and globalisation. Since, the private sector was allowed to operate large scale corporate culture began to acquire commanding heights. The country witnessed fast growth of professional and other new educational institutions where the organizers of these institutions ensure to provide quality education that helps to get placement in companies both within and outside country with high salaries.

Here it should be mentioned that entry or admission into these institutions is not open to all. On the other hand, the entry is restricted to such of those students who can pay high fees and other payments to the managements and Dalits being poor could not find entry into these institutions; they can hope to educate their children in the government institutions where the rule of reservation is being practiced. And the corporate institutions, certainly, have an edge over the Government institutions, in respect of in passing quality education as they do not face resources constraint of any sort. Thus it clearly states that a vast majority of Dalits do not have access to quality education as they do not have the required where-withal to admit their children in the corporate sector institutions.

This fact is further reinforced by the Supreme Court's recent judgement:

The Supreme Court's recent verdict-'No quota in unaided private colleges'-came as a rude shock to the Dalits and other Backward Communities (OBC's). The Supreme Court on 12-08-2005, Friday held that unaided minority and non-minority institutions had absolute rights to admit students of their choice in Medicine, Engineering and other professional courses without Government interference.

A seven-judge Constitution Bench has abolished the State quota and reservation in unaided, private minority and non-minority colleges. The judgment would be effective from the next academic year, 2006-07.

Justice Lahoti writing the unanimous judgment, said, "Merely because the resources of the State in providing professional education are limited, private educational institutions, which intend to provide better professional education, cannot be forced by the state to make admissions available on the basis of (the) reservation policy to less meritorious candidates". (The Hindu, August 13, 2005, Saturday, Banglore Edition).

As a result of this, the Dalits are deprived of quality education and employment opportunity in high profile institutions as the corporate sector is not implementing constitutional provisions for the Dalits.

Although the content of the globalisation openly declares hat the local or the national resources would be used to heighten the global welfare do not speak in favour of the most of the developing countries, like India. For instance, such of those Dalits who were engaged in manufacture and to marketing of foot-wear have to given up there up profession, for they could not be face competition of the international organizations which have advance infrastructural facilities both to manufacture and to marketing a variety of foot-wear across the globe, selling at highly competitive prices. Dalits being poor who use to work with traditional skills produce foot-wear and marketed them in their local areas/sandies are totally vanished from the scene because of the globalisation phenomenon.

From the early 1990's the farmers in India have been enjoying freedom in selection of methods in the process of agricultural production; there were allowed to use all kinds of technologies to modernize their agriculture so as to meet the challenges at the global level. In order to save labour, interalia, the farmers took to rapid mechanization of agriculture, with the use of tractors, threshers, harvesters, crop-tiger and power-driven-sprayers. The skilled and trained labour found jobs leaving behind the unskilled and untrained Dalits without a gainful employment in rural areas and the situation forced them to migrate to cities in search of some job for their survival. This has shattered their families and left them to lead a life in more miserable conditions. The survey that was conducted in Anantapur District revealed the fact that the number of households that belonged of SC's and ST's have increase, significantly in Anantapur city after 1995 onwards; and most of them live in unhygienic slum conditions.

Conclusion

One finds there exists an uneven distribution of wealth in India; nearly, 80 per cent of the wealth owned by the top 20 per cent of the population while 80 per cent of the people command only 20 per cent of the wealth in India. The present Economic Reforms implemented, especially, globalisation was allowed the rich become richer and the poor not becoming better. The Dalits and the OBC's covered under the category of the 80 per cent of the people commanding 20 per cent of the wealth in the country do not hope to improve their Socio-Economic status under privatization and globalisation. Hence, it is imperative to review the existing social security measures intended for the Dalits and OBC's in the country.

The Economic Reforms, Privatisation and Globalisation, instead of improving Dalits and OBC's Socio-Economic status should not allow them to slip down from the existing position.

From the foregone discussion, one sincerely feels that the status of the Dalits and the OBC's seem to have moved from bad to worse during the reforms period in India. Hence, the need of hour is to review and reorient the existing social-security measures to fully safe-guard interests of the Dalits and OBC's in the present and in the ensuing Economic Reforms regime in India.

References

Ganni Raju "The life of Dr. B.R. Ambedkar", Babasaheb Dr. Ambedkar Memorial Society, Hyderabad.

Kerr. Dhananjay, "Dr.Ambedkar: Life and Mission", popular parakasam, Bombay 1987.

Michel, S.M. "Dalits in modern India: Vision and Values", Vistar Publication, New Delhi.

P. Radhakrishnan, E.P.W, Vol. XXVI. No.33, August 17, 1991.

Prem Prakash "Ambedkar Politics and Scheduled Castes", Ashish Publishing house 5, Ansari Road, Darya Ganj, New Delhi-110002.

The Hindu August 13, 2005, Banglore Edition, ISSN 0971-751X, Vol.128, No.192.

Vivek Kumar "Dalit Leadership in India", Kalpaz publications, Delhi-110052.

6

Intellectual Property Rights and Trade Marks

Introduction

The intellectual Property is the product of human mind. Every creation or performance takes its first shape in the mind of a human being and acquires a physical status on the execution of the ideal so conceived. Every mind is not of equal capability or tendency. The differences exist not only in the inherent but also in the acquired qualities. Therefore, the identity of the creator is necessary. This promotes incentive and advances the process of creation in terms of quality as well as quantity. It is in this backdrop that the concept of intellectual property has been developed and has now become popular in the whole world. The term "Intellectual" implies that it is specific to the mind or talent. Looking back in human history the world has advanced through continuous creation of objects and processes by the perpetual exercise of intelligence by different people. Since the nature of the human activities is wide and varied, the creations also very with respect to each activity. In the sphere of law the intellectual property has attained diverse dimensions like: right to reproduce a creation, right to use the creation and the right to make available a product in a particular shape and with a specific label, etc. These rights have come to be known as the copyright, patent, trademark, design, etc. The intellectual property law is thus based on the law of copyright, patents, trade marks and designs. The importance of these rights in the global market, has assumed great significance in recent times particularly after the conclusion of the agreement on Trade Related Intellectual Property Rights (TRIPs).

Formally, the Intellectual property is defined under Article 2 (viii) of the World Property Organization, 1967 to include rights relating to:

- literacy, artistic and scientific works;
- performance of performing artists, phonograms and broadcasts;
- inventions in all fields of human endeavour;
- scientific discoveries;
- industrial designs;
- trade marks, service marks and commercial names and designations;
- Protection against unfair competition and all other rights resulting from intellectual activity in the industrial, scientific, literacy or artistic fields.

The role of intellectual property being of utmost importance in the economic development of a country, it has become inevitably necessary to protect the same. The industrialized nations were therefore exerting tremendous pressure on various countries to provide a stricter set of norms for the protection of intellectual property rights all over the world. Owing to this reason, TRIPs were formulated by the GATT (General Agreement on Tariff and Trade) under the auspices of World Intellectual Property Organization (WIPO).

The most important conventions in respect of the intellectual property are the Paris Convention and the Berne Convention adopted in the year 1883 and 1885 respectively, which was later, revised in 1967. On January 1, 1996, a large number of states viz., 136 became party to the above Convention.

What is Intellectual Property?

Intellectual property is the creation of human mind and human intellect. This is why this kind of property is called 'Intellectual property'. Intellectual property is created by incorporating information in tangible objects capable of multiplying in unlimited number of times at different locations anywhere in the world. The property is basically in the concept, ideal, thought and thereafter is the actual product, work or process, etc.

The World Intellectual Property Organization (WIPO)

provides further clarification on what exactly should be the nature of Intellectual Property. According to WIPO, the Intellectual Property includes rights relating to inventions in all fields of human endeavour, scientific discoveries and industrial designs. It also contains trade marks, service marks and commercial names and designations, literacy, artistic and scientific works and performance of artists, phonograms and alike. Further, the protection against unfair competition and all other rights resulting from intellectual activity in the industrial scientific, literary or artistic fields have been aptly given space in the domain of intellectual property.

IPRs: Pros and Cons in New Trade Regimes

Intellectual Property Rights (IPRs) refer to the legal ownership by a person or business of an invention/discovery attached to a particular product/process, which protects the owner against unauthorized copying or imitation.

A. Types of IPRs: The TRIPs provide the standards and norms on the forms of IPRs as; i) Patents, ii) Copyrights and related rights, iii) Geographical indications, iv) Industrial designs, v) Trademarks, vi) Layout designs of integrated circuits, and vii) Trade secrets (undisclosed information). Further, amongst the different types of TRIPs the legal dimensions concerning the patent particularly and geographical indications to some extent involve the whole lot of discussions.

B. Advantages of IPRs in the New Trade Regime: India contains valuable natural resources and scientific manpower in which IPRs would bring favourable changes to the Indian economy. IPRs indicate massive evidence and reiterate the critical role for productive research and invention. It will also help in increasing percentage of Indian exposure in world trade. Moreover, when patent laws are variant between the trading nations, these give rise to trade and industrial disputes, besides untoward effect on the investment flow. Hence, IPR would protect the Intellectual Property (IP) owners for plagiarism, counterfeiting and other malpractices in time of growing information technology, evolution of global media and communication revolution. The interests of farmers and researchers would be protected through evolving an effective system. This system is a diluted from of patent which provides a favourable framework of plant breeders rights, through which protection is accorded to the researchers and farmers with regard to the use and exchange of seeds and plant genetic material. And lastly, the long period IPRs i.e., patent would also encourage inventions and productive research and India could benefit from such developments.

C. Disadvantages of IPRs in the New Trade Regime: It would promote bio-colonization and legalize monopolies in the form of Multi National Companies (MNCs). There is a chance that many of Indian traditional medicinal plants may get seriously endangered through bio-piracy and over exploitation. The interests of researchers and farmers would be worst hit owing to patenting of seeds of other biological materials. On the other hand accepting product patents in pharmaceutical sector would jerk up the prices of drugs. Extending patents protection period to 20 years would limit access to new technology and production of new product in India and this might promote monopoly practices by the patent holders. Moreover the fear is that MNCs can misuse it to curb competition through wrangling. There is a chance that a strong patent system would impair attempts at development of technology, locally, and more importantly, new patent act is synchronized with TRIPs would virtually render the transition period of 10 years ineffective.

Dimensions of Intellectual Property Rights

1. Patents: Patents are the protection accorded by a government to an inventor for a fixed number of years during which period he will hold full rights to exclude others from exploiting. In return for this right, the inventor discloses details of his innovation to the people. In most countries, patent protection is being given for 20 years from the date of filling. Three basic criteria to be fulfilled for obtaining a patent are novelty, non obviousness and utility.

According to WTO, 1995, a patent is a statutory privilege granted by the government to the inventors and other persons from manufacturing, using or selling a patented product or from utilizing a patented process or method.

Patentable inventions in accordance with the definition of the term, 'invention' has been defined in section 2 (J) of patents Act, 1970, which means any new and useful i) art, process method or manner of manufacture; ii) machines, apparatus, or other article; and iii) substance produced by manufacture.

Therefore, in order to be patentable, an invention must process the characteristics viz., i) It should relate to a manner of manufacture; ii) The manner of manufacture should be novel; iii) It should be outcome of inventive activity; iv) It should have utility; and v) It should not be contrary to law and morality.

2. Industrial Design: An industrial design is an outcome of inventive activity, initially, mentally conceived and then put on a drawing board, followed by the mechanics of giving a concrete shape to the basic new idea in the design and then finally contriving a method for mass manufacturing the same to put forth a product in the market for the benefit of the consumer. A new design thus conceived or invented is, therefore, an intellectual property.

"Design", as defined in the 'Designs Act, 1911', relates only to the features of shape, configurations, pattern or ornamental decoration applied to an article by any industrial process or means. Whether manual, mechanical or even chemical, separate or combined, which in the finished article appeal to and are judged solely by the eye.

3. Trade Mark: Trade marks have been defined as any signs, or any combination of signs capable of distinguishing the goods or services of one undertaking from those of other undertakings. Such distinguishing marks constitute protectable subject matter under the provisions of the agreement. The agreement provides that initial registration and each renewal of registration shall be for a term of not less than 7 years and the registration shall be renewable indefinitely. Compulsory licensing of trade marks is not permitted.

The Indian Trademark Act is in the process of being amended in response to our own requirements. The proposed amendments, if approved, would also bring our trademark law completely in line with our obligation in the TRIPs Agreement. It may be pointed out that by and large the amendments being made in the context of the TRIPs agreement are marginal; the main amendments are in the nature of clarifications and procedural specifications.

4. Copyright: Copyright means all the rights conferred by the Act upon its owner in respect of his literacy, dramatic, musical or artistic work or in respect of cinematographic film or record. It does not only mean the right to do something but also the right to exclude others from committing those acts which are protected under the copyright act. In short, 'copyright' in a work means the exclusive right to do the things specified in it. Thus, copyright secures form of expression and not the ideas or information or opinions. The subject matter of one's imagination or thinking cannot be protected as such. Apart from its form of existence copyright offers protection to original works of authorship in any tangible medium of expression.

5. Layout Designs of Integrated Circuits: The obligation in this area is to comply with the Washington Treaty on layout designs. India is a signatory to the Washington treaty. The main obligations of this treaty which are also incorporated in TRIPs Agreement are the protection of the intellectual property in respect of layout and designs that are original in the sense of feeling the result of their creator's own intellectual efforts and national treatment of foreign right holders. The term of protection is 10 years and the rules in respect of compulsory licensing are the same as in case of patents. India would need to enact legislation to give protection to layout design.

6. Trade Secrets (Undisclosed Information): Trade secrets is defined as "a formula, pattern, device or compilation of information used in one's business and given an opportunity an advantage over competitors who do not know the use of it".

The agreement requires the members to protect the undisclosed information and data submitted to governments or governmental agencies. It also provides that natural and legal persons shall have the possibility of preventing information lawfully within their consent in a manner contrary to honest commercial practices. Further, parties are required to protect against unfair commercial use. Undisclosed or other data obtained as a condition of approving the marketing of pharmaceutical or of agricultural chemical products. In India there is no separate legislation dealing with trade secrets.

Intellectual Property Rights System in India

In a recent study conducted by an NGO, it was revealed that foreign patents were granted more frequently because of India's poor patent literacy and lack of appropriate patent laws. Today United States alone holds 40 patents on products developed from the name and about 50 from other countries, while Indians hold just three. Same is the case of tamarind, while the US holds 30 patents, India has only eight. Similarly, US holds many patents on the plants extensively grown in India, such as "pomegranate" (as antiviral agents), "mustard" and "soapnut" (as fly retardant); "bitter-ground" (treatment of tumours and HIV infection), "amla" (for antiviral activity and hepatitis), "pepper" (Piperin for nutritional use), while India holds too few patents on them. India is taking this whole matter rather casually for which it may have to pay a very high price in future.

As far as physical infrastructure is concerned, the national offices, including the one in New Delhi, are in a decrepit state in both information and infrastructure. It takes a minimum of six years for the complete processing of a patent. There are anything between 20 to 25 thousand pending applications. With just under 40 patent officers, it is possible to clear a maximum of 3,000 applications annually. In such scenario, one wonders if India will be able to overcome this backlog. Feeble moves are afoot to train more patent officers to clear the backlog. Intellectual infrastructure is also growing at a snail's pace. The government is planning to form a joint group consisting of ministries of science and technology, development to boost this vital infrastructure.

In the meantime, organizations facing the brunt of the TRIPs regime have launched their own efforts at creating and strengthening IPR and building databases. Notable among them are the CSIR, Department of Science and Technology (DST), National Research Development Corporation (NRDC), Technology Information Forecasting Assessment Council (TIFAC), Department of Electronics (DOE), National Informatics Centre (NIC), Indian Council of Agricultural Research (ICAR), etc. The Technology promoting NRDC has even introduces an incentive scheme for industries to finance up to 50 per cent and help in filing applications abroad.

Are Indian Decision Makers Prepared to Take Advantage of IPRS Protection?

It seems that India is not ready to take the advantage of the Intellectual Protection Rights regime. Neither has India been able to take stock of resources nor could create an appropriate legal framework to address IPR issues. In the era dominated by WTO. India should look into its potential and try to protect its Intellectual Property by enacting proper legislative measures. In Doha, there was no major gain for India, as the transitional period for ratifying TRIPs agreement for developing countries remained unaltered at 2005, while it was only decided that LDCs could be given an additional time period of 10 years for ratification. The necessity of IPR becomes reality if one thinks in terms of zero tariffs. In the era of globalization, while the whole world is coming under unified market concept, if all tariffs are brought down to zero then "knowledge" becomes only trade differentiator. IPRs give protection to that very important concept of knowledge by offering tools like trademark, copyrights, patent and trade secret and design registration etc.

In the current fast moving world innovation is running faster than our national legal support system. The legal system fails to match product lifecycle with the IPR lifecycle. In USA multinational corporations have been found adopting litigation as a business strategy. By challenging existing "suspect patent" they get them invalidated in the court and utilize the opportunity to capture a good share of the market. There is need to take steps to utilize country's human resources and strengthen the system so that keeping obligation to TRIPs or any other agreements of WTO is less painful. Although patenting of Neem, Haldi and Basmati are much talked about, there are around 65 other items to which patents have been taken. Surprisingly, the patents have been taken on 30 bacterial items collected from Indian soil which are normally not given by attention here as property. But this has failed to wake up our decision makers.

Conclusion

The crux of the Intellectual Property Rights is: to give credit where it is due. With the emergence of the knowledge, society and virtual products, the issue of safeguarding the investment in the information-based products has certainly gained high importance. The people as consumers or producers in the information chain, cannot afford to be ignorant about the IPRs. Thus, the protection of IPRs has definite benefits, such as to propagate innovative culture, profitability and market leadership and helps in creation of wealth for the individual and the nations. Although the world is already on the road to globalization and IPRs agreement in a big way after signing the WTO agreement and the process is irreversible and imminent, the journey is not smooth by any means. There are lots of contentious issues which still need to be addressed and many areas where India and other developing nations are at disadvantage.

There is need to use extensively, the patented and patentable inventions in order to make agriculture and small scale industries viable in the global world. At the same time, the rural economy can also create patentable inventions, particularly those requiring low economic resources. India falling among the developing countries have miles to go, as she has a vulnerable collection of traditional, oral, folklore, customary, agricultural, traditional medicines; but not have much wealth and infrastructure, lack of awareness of IPRs among all strata of people, these are major set backs to a developing country like India.

References

Ghosh, A. (2004), intellectual Property rights-An Imperative Engine for growth", a discussion organized by Consumer Utility &Trust Society, Calcutta.

Kumar, Supran (2004) "WTO and SSIs: Opportunities and threats", Udyog Yug, pp.22.

Mehrotra, (1989), "Patents Act and Technological Self-Reliance: The Indian Pharmaceutical Industry", Economic and Political Weekly, 24 (19), pp.1059-1064.

Nigudkar S. Shruti 'Impact of proposed Changes in IPR on Pharmaceutical Bhat and K.K. Industry', Chemical News December. Maheswari (1997),

Prasad, C.S. (2000), "Implication of WTO on Small Enterprises", Laghu Udyog, Samachar, pp.3.

Rekhi, J.S. (2000), "Importance of intellectual Rights", Laghu Udyog Samachar, pp. 20.

.UN, (1993), "Intellectual Property Rights and Foreign Direct Investment", Transnational Corporation and Management Division Department of Economics and Social Division.

7

Water Resources Management Policies

Introduction

Water Resources Development has been an effective vehicle in ushering the Green Revolution that our country witnessed in Post-Independence era. Irrigated agriculture contributes nearly 56 per cent of the country's agricultural output. In the march of our water resources development and management, we have seen many ups and downs; we have faced many unprecedented challenges successfully. Of late, the nation's attention has been focused on certain issues that have emerged from the development and management of water resources in the country.

The crisis about water resources development and management thus arises because more of the water is not available for use and secondly it is characterised by its highly uneven spatial distribution. Environmentalists like Sunderlal Bahuguna are not wrong in saying that the acute scarcity water may force the powerful nations to wage a new global war for the control of the depleted sources of water. Such a parallel makes the future picture essentially depressing.

India is a victim of uneven spatial distribution of water. For example, the hilly state of Uttaranchal houses several prominent water bodies but thousands of villages in the state still have to do with insufficient water availability. Similarly, despite being a part of the Ganga River basin, Rajasthan suffers from acute water shortage. Therefore, importance of water has to be recognised and greater emphasis laid on its economic use and better management- simply because in our country, inefficient utilization of water has already created a critical situation.

Water Resources

Water is important to the survival of human, plant and animal life. Earth is the only planet in the planetary system endowed with water resources. Nearly 80 per cent of the earth's system is covered with water in the form of oceans, lakes, and rivers etc. The oceans contain most of the water, nearly 97 per cent of the total water and cover most of the water surface on earth. The rest is fresh water and at any time, about 22 per cent of fresh water is stored under the surface of the earth as ground water and the rest is stored in ice caps and glaciers. The water is precious and needs in almost all human activities, irrigation, industry, mining, power generation and domestic and so on.

Table 7.1: Sector-wise Utilisation of Water Resources in India (1997) (per cent)

Domestic	4.9
Industries	3.3
Irrigation	82.9
Power Generation	3.3
Other uses	5.6
Total	100.0

Water Resources Planning

Water resources available to the country should be brought within the category of utilizable resources to the maximum possible extent. Non-conventional methods for utilization of water such as through inter-basin transfers, artificial recharge of ground water and desalination of brackish or sea water as well as traditional water conservation practices like rain water harvesting, need to be practiced to further increase the utilizable water resources. Promotion of frontier research and development, in a focused manner, for these techniques is necessary.

Water resources development and management will have to be planned for a hydrological unit such as drainage basin as a whole or for a sub-basin, multi-sectorally, taking into account surface and ground water for sustainable use incorporating quantity and quality aspects as well as environmental considerations. All individual developmental projects and proposals should be formulated and considered within the framework of such on overall plan keeping in view the existing agreements/awards for a basin or sub-basin so that the best possible combination of options can be selected and sustained.

It present a framework for water policy for sustainable development, and shows how water policy is linked to policies in other sectors, including public finance, agriculture, energy, industry and health, human settlements, transport, and the environment. The intent is to identity the essential elements of a national water policy, while giving only incidental attention to what the content of that policy should be. This attempt may provide some insights to those concerned with formulating new or revised water policies for sustainable development.

Proposed Framework for Water Resources Policy

The item policy is used here to mean a general rule or guideline for decisions or actions in specific case. For example, a typical water resources allocation policy would be one that gives priority to domestic water use in the event of a water shortage. Case-by-case decisions on water allocation would then be guided by this policy. Water policies may show up in various forms, constitutions, laws, administrative regulations, long-range plans and programmes, and budgets. Rarely are such policies neatly codified so that they can be readily identified. Therefore, formulation of the specific elements of a water policy is an essential prerequisite to an assessment of its adequacy and completeness. To this end, a framework for policy analysis is presented here, based on the interrelationship of the three systems. The first of these the natural water resources system, entails the hydrologic cycle the hydrologic cycle, with its components of precipitation, evaporation, surface runoff, and groundwater flows, as well as the broader 'hydrologic continuum', defined by Leopold to include the soil, biota, and atmosphere as well as water. In the aggregate, this system is the water and water- related natural resources endowment or (supply) available for human uses.

The second is the human activity system which is composed of the many human activities that affect, are affected by, the natural water resources system. At one extreme, as in the Nile Valley, people have extensively modified the natural system by constructing storage reservoirs, diversion works, and canals to meet their irrigation needs.

At the other extreme, as in Bangladesh, those inhabiting the floodplains of major streams such as the Ganges and Brahmaputra rivers are at the mercy of natural forces .Between these extremes are works such as stream recession irrigation in West Africa. In the aggregate, these human activities comprise the 'demand' side for water uses such as irrigation, domestic water supply, waste disposal, navigation, hydroelectric power, fisheries, and recreation and for reduction in damages from flooding, water pollution, and drought.

Finally, the water resources management system embodies the activities and relationships in the public and private sectors concerned with harmonizing the supply and demand sides so as to achieve the objectives of the society. In this context, demand includes both uses for water such as for irrigation and domestic needs, and adverse impacts such as pollution arising from human activities, while supply also includes adverse impacts, such as natural floods and droughts, imposed by the water resources system on human activities. An essential support to the water resources management system is the institutional and organizational frame work for management.

In the sections that follow, we will identify those elements of a national water policy that are relevant to each system. An effective water resources policy includes specific elements which

- preserve the integrity of the natural water resource system, and
- provide water and water-related services to people in an economically efficient, equitable, environmentally sound and sustainable manner.

Water Resources Management System

Policies relevant to water resources management are those that guide the planning and implementation of public private programmes and strategies for harmonizing the supply of and demand for water to meet the efficiency, equity and sustainability objectives of society. Examples of such policies are:

1. Establishing unified national objective and priorities for water resources management, including setting guidelines for resolving the inevitable conflicts between national economic growth and self-sufficiency, regional development, equitable income distribution and social impacts, environment quality, and sustainability of the resource base.
2. Developing constructive inter national agreements on water management, which entails equitable sharing of benefits and costs of development/management of international river basins, and clear definition of responsibilities of affected nations.
3. Guiding national investments in water resources development by means of capital investment budgets and programmes, national cost-sharing, international or bilateral grants and/or loans, cost-sharing by provincial, local, and private agencies, and private investment.
4. Adopting projecting formulation and evaluation criteria benefit-cost analysis, risk-assessment analysis and multiple objective analysis to be used for project and program feasibility studies and monitoring and evaluation of performance.
5. Establishment a better balance between development the creation of new projects, such as dams and irrigation systems and management focusing on more efficient use of existing facilities.
6. Planning for involuntary resettlement from development projects, such as storage reservoirs, so as minimize economic and social dislocation, promote development opportunities, and mitigate adverse effects in an equitable manner.
7. Adopting workable approaches to deal with water conflicts

that emphasize negotiation mediation rather than confrontation.

8. Formulating procedures for allocation of water and waste assimilation capacity that take account of interdependency of water uses and the pricing policy. Alternative approaches via water markets with clear property rights versus allocation via planning; or some combination of these two.
9. Establishing standards on centralization versus decentralization of water planning and implementation; for example, reliance on a highly centralized national irrigation or power agency versus regional or local agencies.
10. Promotion public involvement/local participation on project planning and implementation, especially for irrigation, upstream watershed management, rural and urban water supply and sanitation projects.
11. Providing for adequate funding of project operation and maintenance, example from user charges, especially for projects to be turned over to local water users for operation and maintenance.
12. Planning for effective monitoring and ex-post evaluation of projects.

Water Resources Policy Overlaps

The preceding discussion on the elements of a national water policy was without reference to the specific locus of these elements in the national government structure. In face, water resource management is typically divided among a number of government sectors. This means that water policies are not the exclusive domain of a water resource sector but overlap with other sectoral policies, as illustrated in figure. For example, in many countries, the ministry of agriculture has purview over irrigation, and many policies concerning this extremely important water use or established by this agency, other water uses such as hydroelectric power and navigation is the policy domain of ministries of energy and transport. Urban and rural water supply and sanitation are often the concerns of the ministries of health and human settlements while environmental agencies establish policies for water quality and preservation of natural aquatic ecosystems, and forestry agencies are often involved in watershed management activities, which have major repercussions on water resources. In addition, national macro-economic policies on finance and trade can have important impacts on water resource management.

The future of policy overlap in water resources has been analyzing the links between water and other sectors of the economy, including those in agriculture, industry, transport, energy and health. In conceptual framework an overall national water policy entails.

- Policies covering the resources, sector as a whole.
- Policies relating to specific sub-sectors of water resources, such as potable water and irrigation, and
- Policies concerned with other sectors (e.g. energy) hat affect water resources.

Table 7.2: Annual Requirement of Fresh Water in India

S. No	Different uses of water	2000		2025	
		Surface Water	Ground Water	Surface Water	Ground Water
1.	Irrigation	420.0	210.00	510.00	260.00
2.	Other Uses	80.00	40.00	190.00	90.00
A	Domestic and Livestock	32.85		46.00	
B	Industries	30.00		120.00	
C	Thermal Power	3.30		4.00	
D	Miscellaneous	53.85		110.00	

Source: Central Water Commission (W.M. Directorate).

The Table 7.1 explains the annual requirement of fresh water for India in future. Conjunctive use of surface and ground water is very essential to meet the growing future demand for water in

India. Moreover, in future there will be grant pressure on surface water. Hence, sustainable development of water mostly depends on environment friendly management of surface water sources in India.

The contemporary water management exports advocate this idea of sustainable water management should not be difficult for Indians either to accept it or adopt it. To begin with sub-oil water exploitation schemes qualify most for sustainable development strategies. One has to emphasize the reversibility of relationship between crop and sub-oil water. It is water availability that determines the choice of the crop and in the event of a conflict it is the crop that is changed and not the water resource or its supply augmentation.

Conclusion

Based on the framework presented here, the important elements of a water resource policy can be developed on a comprehensive and consistent basis for any specific use. Through our focus is national policies, the approach can be applied also to local, provincial, and international levels.

References

Biswas Jellali and Stout "Water for Sustainable development in the 21st Century, Oxford University Press, Delhi.

Government of India Reassessment of water resources Potential of India, Central water Commission 1993.

Leopold, L.B. "Ethos, Equity and the Water Resource", Environment, Vol.32, No.2, March, pp. 17-20. and 37-42.

Munashinghe, M "water Supply Polices and Issues in Developing Countries, Natural Resource Forum", Vol. 14, No.1, February, pp. 33-48, 1990.

Sahah, Mihir "Water Policy Blues", the Hindu, June 2002.

UNEP "Sustainable Water Development and Management", International Journal of water Resource development, Vol. 5, No. 4, December, pp. 225-251.

8

Interlinking Rivers in India

Introduction

The idea of the 'linking of rivers', dormant for a long time, has acquired new prominence now, particularly in the context of the acute form that the Cauvery dispute has taken, as well as the prevailing drought in several parts of the country. In response to public interest litigation (PIL), the Supreme Court has decreed that the rivers of India shall be linked within ten years, and has directed that a Task Force should be set up for working out the modalities.

Three questions arise: first whether the Supreme Court was right in issuing this direction; secondly, why the Government responded with such clarity and enthusiasm; and thirdly, whether the idea of 'linking of rivers' is a sound one on merits.

There are many different ways in which the future drinking water needs of the people can be met, and the linking of rivers is only one of the ideas mooted in this context. Moreover, it is by n o means clear that there is a direct link between the right to water and the linking of rivers.

The 'human right' to water is invoked in the context of water a life-support, i.e., drinking water. Drinking water is only a small part of total water needs.

The really large demands for water usually, arise in the context of irrigation which accounts for upwards of so per cent of our usable water resources. It is for meeting those huge demands that big project-large dams, long-distance water transfers, the linking of rivers aware mooted. Thus the link with human rights that justifies judicial activism cannot be invoked in aid of a direction for the linking of rivers. The Supreme Court seems to have assumed that the linking of rivers was an accepted idea that has been languishing for decades for want of attention an action.

The linking of rivers did not figure in the Ninth Plan, and so for as one know, the Tenth Plan document now awaiting release does not mention it; a reference may of course be added now. The Report of the National Commission for Integrated Water Resources Development Plan (NCIWRDP) 1999 did not make any major recommendations in this regard; we shall return to this. The Prime Minister's address to the National Water Resources Council (NWRC) commending the National Water Policy (NWP) 2002 for adoption die not refers to it. Thus it is clear that the Government did not have any rivers-linking project on the anvil. The idea is doubtless an old one, but there have always been doubts about its soundness and practicability.

Rationale for Interlinking of Rivers

India is facing the problem of water both in quantity and quality, the rainfall, which is the primary source of fresh water in the country, is confined to 90-100 days of monsoon season. The country receives about 4000 bcm of water as precipitation annually, a large part of which in the Himalayan catchments off the Ganga Brahmaputra-Meghana-Basin.

Cherapunji in Meghalaya as well as in the western of Southern India. The Spatial and temporal variations in t e precipitation over India often lead to immense human sufferings through floods, drought, scarcity of water etc, and the country is affected by drought-food-drought syndrome. Nearly one-third area of the country is drought prone where water is not available even for during purpose during purpose during the summer season. The rationale behind the interlinking tog rivers is based on the view that the r\transfer of water from water surplus river basins to deficit-water river basins would provide a permanent solution to the problem of floods, drought and water scarcity.

Proposed Rivers for Interlinking in India

The Peninsular rivers component involves a number of links of which the most important would be those connecting Mahanadi, Godavari, Krishna, Pennar and Cauvery. The details are given in Table 8.1.

Table 8.1: Linking of Rivers in India

S. No.	Name of Link	From River	To River	Annual volume of Transfer(mm^3)
1.	Manibhadra to Dowleswaram	Mahanadi	Godavari	11,176 (6,500)
2.	Inchampalli to Nagarjunasagar	Godavari	Krishna	16,426 (14,200)
3.	Inchampalli to Pulichintala	Godavari	Krishna	4,371
4.	Polavaram to Vijayawada	Godavari	Krishna	4,903 (3,305)
5.	Almatti to Penner	Krishna	Penner	1,980
6.	Srisailam to Penner	Krishna	Penner	2,310 (2,095)
7.	Nagarjunasagar to Somasila	Krishna	Penner	12,146 (8,648)
8.	Srisailam to Grand Anicut	Penner	Cauvery	8,565 (3,855)
9.	Kattalai Regulater to Vaigai to Gundar	Cauvery	Vaigai	2,252

Source: NCIWRDP's Report, September 1999.

The Himalaya component envisages a number of links that need not be detailed here. The general idea is to transfer water from the Brahmaputra and Ganga systems westwards to southern Uttar Pradesh, Haryana, Punjab, and Rajasthan and perhaps eventually southwards to the peninsular component.

As data relating to the Himalaya Rivers are classified as confidential, even the NCIWRP found it difficult to study these proposals.

1. Kosi-Mechi
2. Kosi-Ghagra
3. Gandak-Ganga
4. Ghagra-Yemuna
5. Sarda-Yemuna
6. Yemuna-Rajasthan
7. Rajasthan-Sabarmathi
8. Chimer-Sone Barrage
9. Spme Dam-Southern Tributaries of Ganga
10. Brahmaputra-Ganga
11. Farraka-Sundaerbans
12. Ganga-Damodar- Subamarekha
13. Subamarekha-Mahanadi

Need for Interlinking of Rivers

The National Water Commission has estimated that the total water requirements of the country in the year 2050 would be about 973 bcm on the lower side and 1180 bcm on the upper side depending upon the actual population growth. However, the Union Ministry of Water resources on the basis of other studies has estimated the 'countries' water requirement to be around 1093 bcm for the year 2025 and about 1447 bcm for the year 2050.

According to the latest world development report (2004) of the World Bank, Delhi and Chennai on the average get barely two hours of water supply daily while cities like Beijing. Hong Kong and Bangkok have nearly 24 hours of water supply. The present utilization from surface and ground water is about 63 per cent and 37 per cent respectively of the total utilized water resources. The present extent and pattern of water utilization for various purposes is an under (Table 8.2).

Since the total water requirement of the country would barely match or may even exceed the present utilizable water resources there is need for both water conservation of what is available and further augmentation of usable water resources.

Table 8.2: Purpose-wise utilization of water resources

Purpose	Present Utilisation (bcm)
Irrigation	501
Domestic	30
Industrial	20
Energy	20
Others	34
Total	605

Source: National Water Development Agency.

The tentative assessment for the future water requirement for various sectors as assessed is presented in Table 8.3.

Table 8.3: Future Demand of Water

Purpose	Year 2010 (bcm)	Year 2025 (bcm)
Irrigation	688	910
Domestic	56	73
Industrial	12	23
Energy	5	15
Others	52	72
Total	813	1093

Source: National Water Development Agency.

Beyond 2025 augmentation of the resources would be imperative through means that are presently conventional.

Since irrigation for agricultural purpose claims major part of available water (around 68 per cent for the country as a whole). There has to be greater efforts in economy and efficiency of water used in the sector. Nearly 51 per cent of irrigation is based on groundwater. The present irrigation efficiency in the country is estimated to be between 30 to 40 per cent and can improves to around 65 to 70 per cent with improved practice.

The cultivable areas of the country are estimated to be about 186 million hectares out of which about 142 million hectares is under cultivation. The production of food grains, which was just about 51 million tones in 1950-1951, has increase to more than 210 million tones at present. This has resulted in the country becoming self-sufficient in food production in the country. With the rise in population and industrialization mounting of more pressure on land is expected that cultivation areas will stabilize at 140-145 million hectares which requires water in sufficient quantity. To meet the water requirement of this cultivable land interlinking of river is necessary.

The safe drinking water is essential for sustenance of life. By March 2000, about 92 per cent of urban population has been covered by safe drinking water. Drinking water requirement of most of mega cities are met from reservoir of irrigation or multipurpose schemes existing nearby or even by long distance transfers.

Only 77 of the 299 class-one cities have 100 per cent water supply coverage. 203 of the 345 class-two towns have low per capita supply of less the 100 liter per capita per day.

Nearly 97 per cent of the total rural habitations have been provided access to the save drinking from nearly 3 million hand pumps and stand-post and about 0.11 million and regional piped water supply schemes. More than 85 per cent of rural water supply is ground water based.

Benefits from the Interlinking of Rivers

The project of interlinking rivers (ILR) in India is expected to provide multidimensional benefits. The expected benefits from ILR are augmentation of irrigation facilities, potable water supply for rural and urban areas, industrial water supply, more generation of hydropower inland navigation, ecological up gradation due to minimum flow guarantee in rivers, sizeable employment generation, flood and drought mitigation, increased tree forming and many other indirect benefits. It is a programme for greeting India, for providing much needed hydropower, for navigation along water ways, for arresting desertification, for water for our parched land, for food, growth, employment and prosperity.

Following benefits are expected to accrue during the implementation and after the completion of the projects:

1. Control of Floods: The country is experiencing severe floods in some pacts while severe drought in some others due to variations in rain falls over time and space. The Brahmaputra and the Ganga rivers carry about 60 per cent of total water resources of the country. The fury of flood causes heavy losses in the entire region of these river valleys and the annual average financial loss approximate Rs. 1,343 crore. The Interlinking project will prove effective in reducing the severity of floods besides causing recharging of ground and under groundwater with the help of canals.

2. Mitigation of Drought: Transfer of surplus water, which runs waste into the sea, from flood prone areas to drought prone areas-especially in Rajasthan and Gujarat, will help to mitigate the severity of drought. An area of about 25 lakh hectare in most of the big states is likely to reap the benefits of drought reduction. The project will also reduce the inequalities in the distribution of renewable water resources and thus reduce the regional imbalance in the availability of water in different river basins of India.

3. Boost to Agri-Business Activities: The interlinking project will help boost the Agri-Business activities such as fisheries, bee keeping, horticulture etc. Of late these activities are attracting the attention of planner's in the wake of globalization. Most of the link canals will be 50 to 100 metre wide more than 6 meter deep. The reservoirs, filled with fresh water would boost the practice of Piciculture and Aquaculture.

4. Expansion of Irrigation Facilities: The ILR will provide additional irrigation facilities to 35 million hectare 25 million hectare surface water and 10 million hectare increased use of ground water apart from the benefits of flood control, drought mitigation, navigation, salinity and pollution control etc. This 35 million hectare of irrigation will be in addition to the ultimate irrigation potential of 140 million hectare.

5. Increase in Hydro Power Generation Capacity: The storage Dams proposed for interlinking of rivers would also generate huge hydropower to the tune of 3,400 MW (Installed capacity).

6. Increase in Domestic and Industrial Water Supply: The interlinking project also proposes to augment domestic and industrial water supply to the metropolitan cities and several other towns and villages enroute of the link canals. These will also facilities inland navigation from the north to the south as most of the link canals would be 100 meter wide and 6 meter deep.

7. Encouragement to Allied Agriculture Activities: The ILR scheme by providing additional irrigation 'facilities to agriculture will not only help increase agricultural production but also enable farmers to raise diversified crops and to undertake allied activities such as dairying, fishing, etc. Irrigated agriculture would also lead to the establishment of agro-industries and some other activities such as transport, marketing, storage, banking, insurance etc. would also be promoted.

8. Increase in Employment Opportunities: Construction of canals, storage dams, long canals, tunnels, cross drainage structures etc. under ILR programme would require huge manpower. Increased demand for construction materials, machinery, equipment etc. will lead to massive industrialization. All these will result in enormous employment opportunities. Besides, implementation of ILR programme will increase intensive agricultural activities with higher crop intensity providing engagement people engaged in agriculture throughout the year.

9. Help in Solving the Problem of Water Scarcity: India is faced with the regime of stress as the per capita availability of water has declined from about 5,177 bcm in 1,951 to 1,869 bcm in 2001. And given the rise in population by 2025, the pre capita availability is likely to drop below 1,000 bcm and this situation will be treated as that of water scarcity. ILR proposal would help in solving this vital problem of water scarcity.

10. Augmentation of Utilizable Water: India receives and annual precipitation of 4,000 bcm out of which 1,869 bcm appears as run off in various river basins. Against this, the utilizable water resources have been estimated at 1,132 bcm. Hence it is necessary to find out ways for augmentation of utilizable water and one important option is the implementation of ILR programme.

Conclusion

Prosperity of the Indian Agriculture lies in the speedy measures taken to interlinking rivers in India. Interlinking of rivers is a social emotional, economic environmental and engineering issue. Politicians in India belonging to different states and parties must rise above the narrow politics feeling and have to show true statesmanship by way of supporting the implementation of the Supreme Court's direction of interlinking rivers in India by 2010, thereby satisfying the water requirements for all the stated purposes to improve the quality of life in the country.

References

Chauhan, B.R. "Settlement of International and Inter-State Water Disputes in India", under the Auspices of the Indian Law Institute, N.M. Tripathi, Pvt. Ltd., Bombay, 1992.

Petrella, Ricardo, "The Water Manifesto", Zed Books, London and Books for change, Banglore, 2001.

Planning Commission Report of the Committee on the Prising of Irrigation Water", New Delhi, 1992.

Ramaswamy R. Iyer "Water Perspectives, Issues, Concerns", 2003, Sage Publications India, Pvt. Ltd B-42, Panchsheel Enclave, New Delhi-11007.

Sir Cyril S Fox "Water", The technical press Ltd, London.

Thomal Dunne and Luna B. Leopold, "Water in Environmental Planning", W.H. Freeman and Company, San Francisco, 1978.

9

Causes of Farmers' Suicides: A Study of Anantapur District

Economic Reforms and Agriculture in India

It is pertinent to recall as Statement from the Tenth Five year plan document, which says that "Agricultural Development is central to economic development of the country "The share of the agriculture in National Income came down to 22.1 per cent for the year 2002-03 from 55.4 per cent in 1950-51. Although its share in the country's GDP gradually declining, but its hold on catering to the employment needs of the country is quite significant; it provides employment to around 65 per cent of the told work force in the country.

The New Economic Reforms (NER) implemented in the country from 1991 to put the country on the fast track of economic development. In reality, experience over a period of 15 years, reveals that the NER seem to have not developed the country as anticipated. For the agriculture sector faced a severe crisis in Tamil Nadu, Maharastra, Punjab and Andhra Pradesh resulting in large number of farmers suicides.

The major factors at macro level are liberalization privatization and Globalization. It has been observed that agriculture development policies and economic reforms have led to a phenomenal rise input costs which manifested in the forms of "Removal of subsides on fertilizer and pesticides. The supply of fertilizers has been handed over to private agents. The government has withdrawn from the supply of certified quality seeds and fertilizers and pesticides. There is high use of pesticides and fertilizers, increasing farmer's costs but not their yield. Added to this, the cost of credit has enormously increased, specially, after the implementing of the Narasimham Committee report. As a result, the banks stopped financing agriculture and the small – Scale industry as priority sectors for lending at low cost interest rates. As such the farmers have been forced to approach private's money lenders who charged high rates of interest ranging from 60 per cent to 120 per cent, with terms often taking hold of the title deed of the land.

Reasons for the Crisis

As a part of NER, the Government withdrew from supplying quality pesticides, fertilizers and extension services and it was entrusted to be provided by private parties and there were no regulations to oversee these activities of the private parties in these spheres of activity. This situation gave a scope for marketing of spurious seeds pesticides and fertilizers. Farmers, in good faith purchased all these inputs which were found spurious and thus landed them up in untold miseries.

As a part of trade liberalization, the Indian farmers were allowed to export of raw cotton. This in the early 1990's enabled the farmers to earn good returns. And this enticed other farmers to fallow suit. Meanwhile, the advanced countries have highly subsidiaries agriculture sector, resulted in quantum jump in the cotton – production. As result, the cotton prices come down rather sharply in the international market. This had adversely affected the agricultural prospects of the Indian farmers who recently took up cotton cultivation. The increase in the cost of production of cotton and sharp decline in the prices at international level landed the Indian farmers in the crises.

Even in the case of wheat cultivation the support price is fixed at Rs. 650 per Quintal. The farmers and their associations have made prevent plea to the government to enhance the support price of wheat by another Rs. 200 per Quintal. Since the government did not enhance the support price of wheat, the procurement target could not be reached inspite of the fact that there was no dearth of required quantity of wheat within the country. Indeed, it sounds rather strange that in order to meet procurement target the Government in reported to have imported wheat at a price of Rs. 1,200 per Quintal. In a context like this, the farming community looks up to government to ensure sustainability.

During the last 10 year, the farmers' suicides reached to a record number of 1.40 lakh. And in the last three years the farmer's suicides recorded to be 3,500 in the state of Andhra Pradesh

Causes of Farmers' Suicides

It is learned that the following are the chief reasons for farmers' suicides:

1. Crop failure,
2. Failure of irrigations sources, such as wells and bore wells.
3. Lack of remunerative prices for agricultural products.
4. Crop losses due to fake seeds
5. Mounting domestic expenses
6. Ill health of wife and farmer himself
7. Marriage expenses of son or daughter
8. Loss from leased in land;
9. Gambling and addicted to alcohol
10. Involvement in politics.

The maximum number of farmers reported to have committed suicide because of the listed reasons from 1 to 8, and an insignificant number of farmers reported to have committed to suicides on the basis of listed reasons 9 and 10.

Farmers' Suicides in Anantapur District

Anantapur is the largest district in Andhra Pradesh in terms of geographical area, 19,130 sq Km and comprises a population of 36.39 lakh according to 2001 censes. The district receives the lowest average annual rainfall of 544 mm in the state and it is known for recurring droughts and large scales seasonal migration to the neighboring districts/states. The district is relatively backward in terms of literacy rate at 57 per cent when compared to the sate average of 61 per cent for the population aged 7 years and above according to the 2001 censes. The district has thin forest cover (10 per cent of the geographical areas, and the net irrigated area formed hardly 15 per cent of the net sown area. The main sources of irrigation is wells/bore wells, accounting for about 72 per cent of the net irrigated area followed by canals 22 per cent and ponds/tanks and other sources the rest.

Groundnut is the principal crop grown in the district accounting for over 71 per cent of the gross cropped area. The other principal crops of some significance are paddy (5.7 per cent), and jowar (3.2 per cent). Besides groundnut, the other important commercial crops grown in the district are mulberry, sweet orange, papaya, pomegranate, grape and mango. The district has experienced recurring droughts as a result of both scanty and erratic rainfall, lending to crop loss in respect of all the major crops. The agricultural economy of the district moves around the groundnut cultivation. There has been a failure of groundnut crop for four successive years from 2000 to 2003-04, causing untold miseries to the farming community. In addition, the water table had gone down considerably and farmers had gone for more and more number of bore wells to save the standing commercial crops on which they pinned their hopes to get good returns. There has been some prospect for the farmers during 2004-05 as they obtained relatively good crop of groundnut in the district

The farmers' suicides were reported in 60 out of 63 mandals in Anantapur district. The Division-wise farmers' suicides in Anantapur district between 08-12-1998 to 16-1-2006 have been presented in Table 9.1. According to the Table, Anantapur revenue division accounted for 51 per cent of the farmers' suicides in the districts followed by penukonda (30 per cent) and Dharmavaram (19 per cent) divisions. The stratification of farmers suicides on the basis of caste revealed that 49 per cent of the farmers' belonged to OC Category followed by BC (42 per cent) SC (5 per cent) and ST (4 per cent) categories.

The Mandal – Wise farmers' suicides in Anantapur Revenue Division have been presented in Table 9.2; it explains that in two Mandals viz., Singanamala and Guntakal accounted for one each of farmers suicide, while kudair accounted for one each of farmers' suicide, while kudair accounted for 16 followed by 15 in Garladenna; 14 B.K. samudram; 13 Anantapur; 12 Atmakur;

Rapthadu and Tadpatri 12 each; and 11 in Narpala.

Table 9.1: Division-wise Farmers' Suicides in Anantapur District from 08-12-98 to 01-06-06

Sl. No	Division	OC	BC	SC	ST	Total	Per cent
1.	Anantapur	79	77	05	05	166	51
2.	Dharmavaram	29	25	07	02	63	19
3.	Penukonda	51	34	05	07	97	30
	Total Percentage	159 49	136 42	17 05	14 04	326 -	100

Nine out of 20 Mandals in Anantapur Revenue Division have accounted more than 10 farmers' suicide in each Mandal. Thus, accounting for the highest number of farmers' suicides in Anantapur district as a whole.

In the case Penukonda Revenue Division, Roddam Mandal alone accounted for 11 farmers' suicides followed by 7 each in Mandals of Madakasira and Gudibanda and six each in the case of Amarapuram, Penukonda and Thanekal. It is significant note that farmers' suicide cases have been registered in all the 23 mandals of the division.

According to the Table 9.2 Dharmavaram Revenue Division accounted for the lowest number of farmers` suicides in the district. However, C.K. Palli Mandal registered 8 farmers` suicides followed by 6 each in the case of Bhramhasamudram and kanekal; and 5 each in Bathalapalli, Beluguppa, Kalyanadurg and kambadur; and 4 each in the case of Dharmavaram and kanaganapalli.

Thus, it can be conclusively started that Anantapur Revenue Division accounted for the highest number of suicides (166) followed by penukonda (93) Dharmavaram (63) during the period under reference.

The division-wise compensation distributed to the kin of the farmers' suicide has been fixed at Rs. 50,000.

Table 9.2: Mandal-wise Farmers' Suicide Cases: Penukonda Revenue Division

Sl. No	Mandal Name	OC	BC	SC	ST	Total
1.	Agali	02	-	-	-	02
2.	Amadagur	01	01	-	01	03
3.	Amarapuram	06	-	-	-	06
4.	Bukkapatnam	01	01	-	-	02
5.	Gandlapenta	02	-	-	02	04
6.	Gorantla	01	03	-	02	06
7.	Gudibanda	04	03	-	-	07
8.	Kadiri	02	02	-	-	04
9.	Kothacheruvu	03	01	01	-	05
10.	Madakasira	02	04	01	-	07
11.	Mudigubba	04	01	-	-	05
12.	Nallacheruvu	02	-	-	01	03
13.	Nallamada	02	01	-	-	03
14.	Nambuli pulakunta	02	-	-	01	03
15.	Obuladevi cheruvu	-	01	-	-	01
16.	Parigi	-	02	-	-	02
17.	Penukonda	06	-	-		06
18.	Puttapatri	-	02	-	-	02
19.	Roddam	04	06	01	-	11
20.	Rolla	-	02	-	-	02
21.	Somandepalle	01	01	01	-	03
22.	Talupula	02	02	-	-	04
23.	Tanakal	04	01	01	-	06
	Total	51	34	05	07	97

Source: Collectarate, Anantapur.

Since more number of females, suicide in Anantapur Revenue Division, the highest compensation amount of Rs. 103.59 lakh was distributed among 166 legal heirs of the farmers who have committed suicide, while in the case of Penukonda it was Rs. 44.20 lakh, distributed among 99 household and it was only Rs.30.50 lakh in the case of Dharmavaram Revenue Division distributed among 63 households, vide Table 9.3.

Table 9.3: Division-wise Compensation Distributed among the Legal Heirs of the Farmers who Committed Suicide in Anantapur District (Rs. lakh)

Sl. No	Division	SC	ST	BC	OC	Total
1.	Anantapur	2.50	2.50	38.17	60.42	103.59
2.	Dharmavaram	3.21	1.00	11.79	14.50	30.50
3.	Penukonda	1.77	3.26	15.48	23.72	44.23
Total		7.48	6.76	65.44	98.64	178.32

The Division-wise farmers' suicides cases reported during the pre and post date of 14-05-2004, the date on which the present Government came to power in the state, has been displayed in Table 9.4. It is learned from the table that the farmers' suicides prior to May 14, 2004 were 197 while during the post period of 14-05-2004 to till date (July 9, 2006) reported to be 129 farmers' suicide cases in Anantapur District. It is inferred that the farmers' suicides have progressively came down, rather sharply in the post period. It is all due to the state Governments' positive and effective measures through Help-Line and other means to extend the needed financial assistance to both farmers who have committed suicide and those farmers who were reported to be in distress conditions.

Conclusion

It is true that the contribution of agricultural sector to the nations' GDP Is only 22.5 per cent; but 65 per cent of the work-force derives sustenance from the agricultural sector. Keeping this in view, the union Government, should suitably increase the

Budgetary allocations to the agriculture sector so as to provide all the necessary infrastructure, such as, assured irrigation, quality seeds, pesticides, fertilizers, cold-storages, marketing facilities through support price and access to the latest technologies to increase to productivity levels, in addition to subsidies to save farmers from the distress conditions. The farmers require finances at low interest rate not only for agriculture purposes but also for education housing and to celebrate marriage of their daughter/son. The Government may arrange a package of financial assistance even to meet the social obligations as in the case of vidarbha in Maharastra, where the government arranged to provide a Mangalasutram, a gas - cylinder and some vessels totally worth of Rs. 10,000.

Table 9.4: Division-wise Farmers' Suicide Cases during the Pre- and Post-periods of May 14, 2004 in Anantapur District

S. No	Division	Pre period	Post period	Total
1.	Anantapur	97	69	166
2.	Dharmavaram	33	30	63
3.	Penukonda	67	30	97
	Total	197	129	326

Source: Collectarate, Anantapur.

Suggestions

As is evident from the study that the state governments' efforts could effectively bring down farmers suicides from May 14, 2004 the state Government May take all the necessary steps to save farmers from distress by way of immediately announcing and implementing a new package of assistance based on the recently announced central assistance of Rs. 15,000 crore to better the conditions at the farmers in the state of A.P. which act may embolden the forming community to squarely face the situation and thus save their lives from committing suicides in the district.

In this context Government may take all the necessary steps including, crop insurance and complete all the irrigation works for which the present government has laid foundation stones which includes Handri-Niva project. And also extend the provision of input subsidy and simultaneous development of sectors like, animal husbandry, horticulture, sericulture, poultry and handlooms in the district of Anantapur.

References

Eenadu, Anantapur edition, dated 08-07-2006.

Government of Andhra Pradesh, Five Year Plan documents Hyderabad.

Government of Andhra Pradesh, Season and Crop report–2004, Hyderabad.

Government of Andhra Pradesh, Statistical Abstract–2004&2005, Hyderabad.

Government of India, Five Year plan documents, New Delhi.

Government of India, Yojana, March 2006 Publication Division, Yojana Bhavan, New Delhi.

Kasturi & Sons Limited, Front line, July 14, 2006, Vol: 23, No: 3, National Press Chennaiah.

The Hindu, Bangalore edition dated 01-07-2006 & 08-07-2006.

Part II: Industrial Development, Infrastructure and Regional Disparities

By
G. Satyanarayana
M.L. Kantha Rao
M. Reddi Ramu
M.V. Raghavulu
I. Sreenivasulu

10

Industrial Development of Anantapur District

The purpose of this paper is to assess the economic potential of Anantapur district and explore the ways of preventing it from the possible desertification by suitable development of entrepreneurial abilities.

An Overview of the Economy of Andhra Pradesh

The district of Anantapur has been declared chronically drought- affected in the state of A.P. It was one of the six districts in the India selected by the World Bank of special assistance in 1970's. The chief causative factor for the backwardness of agriculture in the district is its geographical location in the centre of the peninsula, which renders it the driest part of the state of the state. Being far away from the east coast, it does not get the full benefit of the North-East monsoons and being cut off by the high Western Ghats, the South-West monsoons are also prevented from penetrating and quenching the thirst of the parched soil. Thus, it is located in a rain shadow area of the state.

Drought and famine has become a recurrent feature in the district. It is observed that during the preceding 35 years drought and famines have frequented the district on an average once in two years. In fact, 1985-86 was the second consecutive year of severe drought, which resulted in crop failure and caused a serious scarcity of food and fodder. The period also witnessed a heavy loss or cattle population in the district.

In 1981 the annual rainfall in the district was 544 mm as against 672 mm and 898 mm for Rayalaseema and Andhra Pradesh, respectively. The rainfall in the district is not only scanty but uneven and uncertain with a high coefficient for raising any crop successfully. Wells, bore wells, tanks and canals from the chief sources, viz., rivers, have severely limited the irrigation development in the district. The existing water sources of water for cultivation. Absence of perennial water sources, viz., rivers, has severely limited the irrigation development in the district. The existing water sources provide irrigation facilities only to 17.34 per cent of the gross cultivated area in the district as against the corresponding gross irrigated area of 21.9 per cent and 35.4 per cent for Rayalaseema and Andhra Pradesh, respectively. Thus, a vast portion of cultivable land is left to the vagaries of monsoons, which very often end up in failure.

Red soils are predominant outside Gooty and Tadipatri taluks. About two-thirds of the area in Hindupur and Madakasira taluks is covered with fertile red loams. But otherwise in the rest of the taluks which have preponderance of red soils, it has been said that, 'the poverty of upland soils beggar description'. Of all this miserable area, Kalyandurg is the most wretched.

Of the total cropped area 69.3 per cent is under food crops and 30.7 per cent is under non-food crops. The area under paddy in the district constitutes only 6.1 per cent of area under food crops. The principal crops of the district are jowar, ragi, bajra and other cereals and millets. In Rayalaseema, Anantapur district has the largest proportion of area under pulses. The principal non-food crops in the district are groundnut and cotton. Groundnut accounts for as much as 24 per cent of the total cropped area. The yield rate even in respect of this crop is poor.

With modern seeds requiring greater investment on fertilizer, water, tools, implements and plant protection measures etc., the small farmer is forced into debts, and if his land fails him his back is broken and he is forced even to give up his ancestral land and profession, he is forced to became a rickshaw puller, a shoeshine boy, a smuggler or a thief in cities. The agrarian picture obtaining in Anantapur district is not different from the general scene described above.

Though in respect of cultivable area per agricultural worker, Anantapur district ranked first (1971), in respect of per capita rural population gross value of output it occupied the ninth rank.

It is thus obvious that through the cultivated area is more, the net benefit is less.

It is, therefore, extremely necessary to develop alternative occupations in the non-farm sector, say, through industrialization, as, it is normally believed that industrialization solves the problems of non-employment, insecurity and poverty. The battle against drought and famine in the district hinges upon creating locally subsistence or secure employment in industry.

However, that the district is industrially backward can be seen from following facts: In the case of number of factory workers, per lakh of population, Anantapur ranked 18 among the 21 districts in the State; in respect of industrial establishments using electricity, it ranked 8; and in respect of per capita consumption of electricity it ranked 13.

Resource Position

Though the district is backward in general, it has the advantage in production of some of the agricultural outputs which could be used as inputs in industrial sector. The districts stands third in the state of Andhra Pradesh in the production of quality oil seeds, chiefly, groundnut oil seeds, cotton and onions; first in coriander and mulberry.

The district has congenial climate for cultivation of mulberry. The area under mulberry cultivation increased to 58,460 acres by the end of 1985-86 fro 1,096 acres in 1975-76. The production of cocoons during 1982-83 was 96.67 lakh tones, worth Rs. 2,783.64 lakh. There is a vast potential in the district for mulberry cultivation. The speed with which sericulture has spread in the district is proof of the dynamism of the Anantapur citizen and his willingness to seize and good opportunity by its forelock.

Coming to mineral resources, in spite of the comparative preeminence of Cuddapah and Kurnool districts in mineral production, Anantapur can still be regarded as a district of minerals. Thus, steatite which Cuddapah does not produce and gold which is mined neither in Cuddapah nor Kurnool are found in this district at Ramagiri on a substantial scale. The district stands first and second respectively in having a large number of goats and sheep. Thus, wool and skins of goats and sheep are available in large quantities. A fair degree of infrastructural facilities are also available in the district for industrial development. By the end of 1985 there were 197 branches of commercial banks spread all over the district. Banking facilities are available generally to industrial units in their respective local areas.

Industries in the District

Though the need for industrialization was felt long back, the existing large and medium scale industries in the district are of recent origin. At the time of independence, accepting J.R.S. Textile Mills, no other industry worth the name existed in the district. It was only during the latter half of the present century that a modest beginning was made with the assistance of District Industries Centre (DIC). The DIC is an official organization which came into being in November, 1978 with a view to providing all essential facilities for promotion and development of industries, especially small scale, village and cottage industries in the rural areas. With the assistance of DIC at Anantapur, industries began to come up in the district. By the end of 1984-85, the number of large and medium scale industries rose to 11 from 3 in 1968, with a capital investment of Rs. 2,904 lakh. They provided employment to 4,956 workers. During the same period the small scale industries went up to 1,435, with a capital investment of Rs. 611 lakh and provided employment to 9,325 workers.

Entrepreneurship in the District

The entrepreneurial culture did not develop fast in the past to accelerate the process of industrialization in the district. Perhaps, the entrepreneurial ability was not dry but shy. The shy, the hesitant and the halting entrepreneurial ability available in the district has to be properly encouraged to take greater risks. For this, oral advice and precept alone may not help. Material and technical support has to be provided at the institutional level by the Governments concerned.

The sound resource base is not always a prerequisite for industrial development or its presence a sure way to prosperity. Bihar is backward in spite of rich mineral wealth within itself; on the other hand, Japan has a major share in International market for steel through there are no iron and steel mines in it. So given the political will and public enthusiasm, industries can be started in Anantapur district in big way.

A majority of the large and medium scale industries are being owned and managed by people who are immigrants to this district. The immigrants have switched over to industries after the nationalization of their bus routes in A.P. Lightings Limited, Anantapur, a joint venture project, an entrepreneur from Anantapur district participated with the Government of A.P. in the production of electric bulbs. So, there is need to foster industrial culture in the district.

In this context a broad survey conducted in the three blocks of Anantapur district, viz., Hindupur, Kudair and Uravakonda to assess the emerging pattern of entrepreneurs in the small scale industries revealed the fact that in the first two blocks non-farming communities, such as Vyayas and Muslims have been managing 67 per cent of the sample units; whereas in Uravakonda 50 per cent of the sample units have been managed by weaving community people. This was the effect of decline in demand for traditional cotton fabrics consequent on the diversification of occupational pattern.

It was noted that in all the three blocks surveyed, entrepreneurs with agricultural background are a non-existing class; perhaps, this is due to subsistence nature of agricultural economy in the district.

It is a matter of satisfaction that there is concentration of entrepreneurs in the district in places, like Anantapur town, Dharmavaram, Hindupur, Rayadurg, Guntakal and Kadiri. But most of them had been engaged in simple and easy ways of earning through maintenance of transport equipment-lorries and taxis and Finance Corporations. All these persons have to be persuaded to take up new lines of production, because it helps in the development of the district.

The level of industrial development in a district or a region among other things is largely a function of supply of entrepreneurs. It is, therefore, imperative to encourage and promote the existing and prospective class of entrepreneurs through attractive intensives. This can be achieved through the following measures:

1. It calls for reorientation of the present industrial policy so as to attract enough number of entrepreneurs in this context of the development of this backward district. Because the current subsidies and concessions fail to accomplish fully the object of attaining rapid industrialization in the district.
2. Establishment of industrial training Institutions (ITIs) is emphasized, at least on a temporary basis, one each at Dharmavaram, Hindupur, Kadiri, Guntakal and Madakasira, to impart technical skills which enable them either to seek jobs in industrial sector or to establish industrial units individually. Above all, it will go a long way in spreading the message of self-employment in every nook and corner of the district.
3. Banks may be instructed by the Governments to be liberal and avoid delays in disbursing loans to industrialists. Instructions should also be issued to banks not to insist upon surety. For it is reported that many a cottage industrial unit owner fails to get bank loans for want of surety.
4. Adequate quantity and quality of scarce raw materials, at reasonable prices, need to be supplied on a sustained basis.
5. Governments, the Union and the State, need to protect and patronize the industries that would be established in the backward areas.

Industrial Potential

Most of the resources available in the district, even today, are exported, either in the semi-processed or raw form. It is due to absence of industries which could make use of them. For example, only 20 per cent mulberry cocoons produced in the district are being processed for their final use of the looms, while 25,000 silk looms (according to an estimate) buy processed silk worth Rs. 100 crore per annum in Bangalore market. Five Spinning Mills, largely cater to the needs of textile mills outside district. There is ample scope for establishment of two textiles mills, one each at Hindupur and Guntakal.

Installation of modern wool carding units at. Penukonda, Madakasira, Kambadur and Rayadurg, the places of concentration of the traditional crumbly weaving and sheep rearing communities, will promote and develop their occupational skills.

Industrialisation or Desertification

If, the agriculturally backward and industrially poor Anantapur district is to be saved from impending desertification, in spite of the existence of the not unsatisfactory human and physical resource base, the Union and State Governments should flood the district with heavy investment and start industries, particularly, assembling, ancillary and foot-loose industries. If the deserts of Rajasthan can be made to blossom by bringing in the waters of Sutluj, that of preventing possible desertification and the semi-arid district of Anantapur should not be difficult. So, for the children of J.A. Schumpeter, Anantapur district poses a challenge.

References

Anantapur Industrial Opportunities, 1972, pp.17-22.

D.S. Bawa, industrial Development of Flood and drought Prone Areas, New Delhi, 1978, p.158.

Data News Feature, Andhra Pradesh, Year Book, 1984, Hyderabad, p.342.

Deputy Director of Sericulture, A Narrative Report of the Sericulture in Anantapur district, 1985-86, p.317.

DIC-Report of 1984-85, Anantapur.

District Collectorate, Department of Industries.

Government of Andhra Pradesh, District Gazetteers-Anantapur district (Revised edition), Hyderabad, 1970, p.317.

Government of Andhra Pradesh, District Gazetteers-Anantapur district (Revised edition), Hyderabad, 1970, p.330.

Government of Andhra Pradesh, Fifth Five Year Plan, Hyderabad, 1973,

p.604.
Government of Andhra Pradesh, Fifth Five Year Plan, Hyderabad, 1973, p.568.
Statistical Abstract, Andhra Pradesh., Hyderabad, 1981, p.57.
The Hindu, February 1986.

11

Cottage and Small Scale Industries under Five Year Plans

The Fiscal Commission of 1945-50, has defined a cottage industry is "one which is carried on wholly or primarily with the help of the members of the family either as a small-scale industry is "one which is operated mainly with hired-labour, usually with 10 to 50 hands and not carried on in the cottage of the worker as the resources of the producer are limited1. It included all those industrial units or establishments whose capital investment of less than 35 lakh rupees (as per the investment criterion for small-scale industrial units in 1985).

India is traditionally known for her small scale and cottage industries. During the 17th century, India is hub of world commerce and magnet of world precious-metal. Europe had to pay mainly in bullion for the increase in the volume of Indian exports. In several handicrafts, the specialization of jobs had advanced to such an extent that a particular class of artisans undertook district process in the chain of production commanded wide foreign markets.

The strategy of village and small scale industries development approach was adopted in the Five Year Plans, especially, in the Second Five Year Plan.

Karve Committee

The Planning Commission appointed a committee in June 1955, viz., 'Karve Committee', to look in to the problems of the village and small scale industries. The committee suggested "to build up a pyramidal structure of industry board based on progressive rural economy through small industrial units also with the necessary services in big villages and small towns all over the country2". The Committee also suggested the need for positive measures of assistance through dissemination of technology and skills for the development of traditional rural industries.

The kadhi and village industries commission was established in April 1957 with more executive powers of planning organization and implementation of the programme for the development of village industries.

For the development of small scale industries, "Industrial Estate Programme" was started in 1955. It offers sheds, work-shops, water power, and other common facilities for rapid small scale industries development. Through 120 new industrial Estates have sanctioned for the plan period only 60 industrial estates came into being comprising 700 small factories in the country.

Ashok Mehta Committee (AMC) (1966)

The Ashok Mehta Committee (AMC), which was popularly known as 'khadi and village industries Committee', was constituted to suggest suitable measures for the fast development of village and small scale industries in India. The Committee suggested a seven year programme for progressive improvement of techniques in respect of each of the traditional industries, including khadi. The committee also recommended additional production of traditional and amber khadi on self sufficiency basis and for introduction of Power where necessary. It also recommended christening khadi and village industries commission as rural industries commission (RIC) to cover all vital aspects which were needed to give to big boost to rural industries in the country.

The main objective of the district industries centre (DIC) programme was to create industrial culture among the realties by providing them with the necessary training facilities to promote self-employment with in the village and thus reduce the migration of village to urban areas. The programme of international rural development programme (IRDP) was formed with the components of programme like RIP, SFDA, and DPAP etc. The programme was implemented during the year1978-79. The trust of the programme was to lift as many rural people as possible above the poverty full employment during agricultural lean period. The landless agricultural labourer's share-croppers and rural artisans would be covered under this programme. Under this scheme financial assistance in the form of subsidy and margin money would be made available to the targeted groups by different financial institutions.

During the six five year plan period of 1980-85 the scheme of 'Area Development programme' was accorded the top priority. In an attempt to achieve the goal of area development the planning commission endorsed the formulation and implementation of new schemes like NREP, TRYSEM AND RLEGP. The sixth five year plan contemplated a substantial improvements of skills and introduction of appropriate technology etc. Greater weightage has been laid on artisans and small entrepreneurs. The employment levels have been estimated to go up to 19.5 millions in 1970-803.

The Sixth Plan outlay was of the order of Rs. 97, 500 crore of which Rs.1,780 crore, accounted for 1.9 per cent of the total plan outlay was allotted to extend financial assistance for the development of village and small scale industries in the country.

The Seventh Five Year Plan laid down the following objectives for the village and small scale industries:

1. to assist in the growth and wide dispersal of industries;
2. to increase the level of earnings of artisans;
3. to ensure regular supply of goods and services through use of local skills and resources; and
4. to develop entrepreneurship with the combination of improved methods of production.

The total outlay of the Seventh Five Year Plan was the order of Rs. 1, 80,000 crore of which only Rs. 2,752.5 crore accounted for 1.5 per cent of the total plan outlay was allocated for the development of village and small scale industries. A considerable progress was recorded in certain aspects viz., employment, production and exports of products of village and small scale industries during the Seventh Five Year Plan.

During the Seventh Five Year Plan significant efforts were made to provide better employment opportunities. The employment position in the village and small scale industries during 1984-85 was 309 lakh and rose to 385 lakh in 1989-90, signifying a compound growth rate of 4.4 per cent.

Eighth Five Year Plan

Owing to the political instability that prevailed at the Centre, Eighth Five Year Plan could not be launched immediately after the Seventh Five Year Plan. This necessitated for the formation of the two annual plans for the years 1990-91 and 1991-92.

The Eighth Five Year Plan (1992-97) aimed to achieve 5.6 per cent annual growth rate in respect of gross domestic product. The plan laid a considerable emphasis for the promotion and development of rural industries on a massive scale.

While endorsing the approach and strategy that was followed during Sixth and seventh plan periods to tackle the problems of rural development and alleviation of rural poverty, the Eighth Five Year Plan made a bold attempt in finding solutions to the problems. In order to achieve the goals set for the eighth Five Year Plan the government designed a suitable policy with the following specific objectives.

1. To increase participation of the people in the rural development process;
2. To decentralize the planning process;
3. To effectively enforcement of the land reforms; and
4. To provide greater access to credit.

The total outlay of the Eighth five Year Plan is of the order of Rs. 7,98,000 crore of which public sector outlay Rs. 4,34,000 crore accounting for 54.39 per cent with Rs. 3,61,000 crore in fresh investment and Rs. 73,000 crore as current expenditure. The total public sector outlay n industry and minerals at 1991-92 prices is Rs. 44,337 corers; of which, Rs. 34,842 crore will be contributed by the central Government and Rs.9,494 crore by the State Government and Union Teritories.4 That means, the Centre and the state governments would be 78.58 and 21.42 respectively. Of the total outlay of indust4y and mineral sector, the outlay on the village and small scale industries will be Rs. 4,778 crore, which will be shared be 2,320 crors.5 that means, the share of percentage for the Centre; and the States and Union Territories is 51, 44 and 48.56 respectively. It is, obvious, that out of the total public sector outlay, the percentage share of investment for village and small scale industries and minerals is 1.32 and 12.28 respectively. But even among the industry and minerals under the public sector, the total allocation for village and small scale industries in 10.78 per cent. Since employment is the antidote for rural poverty the Government of India determined to continue to extend assistance for the ongoing schemes such as IRDP, TRYSEM, and JRY which are specially designed to lift as many people as possible above the poverty line even during the Eighth Five Year Plan period.

In recognition of the positive merits of village and small scale industrial units, the government of India had been striving through successes five Years Plans to develop them on a massive scale (Table 11.1).

Table 11.1: Financial Allocation for Village and Small-scale Industries (VSSI) under the Five Year Plans

Plan	Period of Years	Total Outlay	VSSI	% of VSSI from total outlay
Ist Plan	1951-56	1,960	42.0	2.1
2nd Plan	1956-61	4,672	187.0	4.0
3rd Plan	1961-66	8,577	241.0	2.8
Annual Plans	1966-69	6,625	126.0	1.9
4th Plan	1969-74	15,779	243.0	1.9
5th Plan	1974-79	39,426	592.0	1.5
6th Plan	1980-85	97,500	1,780.0	1.8
7th Plan	1985-90	1,80,000	2,753.0	1.5
8th Plan	1992-97	3,61,000	4,778.0	1.3

Source: 1. Statistical Outline of India, 1986-87. 2. The seventh five year Plan (1985-90). 3. Eighth Five year Plan (1992-97).

Promotional Efforts

The Government of India has set up a number of promotional agencies, such as small Scale Industries board, the Khadi and Village Industries Commission, All India Handicrafts board, the All India Handloom board, the Coir Board and Central Silk board. In order to encourage the small sector, the Central Government had initially reserved 180 items to be exclusively produced in village and small scale industrial sector. It is significant to note that the list has been enlarged to 504 items (according to the IPR 1977).

To provide institutional credit to this sector, financial assistance is made available through the concerned State Government through State Financial Corporation and Commercial Banks. The provision of Refinance facilities are arranged trough the **NABARD.**

Technical advice and assistance to small scale manufactures is provided by Small Industries Development Organization (SIDO) through its service centres, production and training centers.

Problems and Prospects

Despite the fact that the Union Government is trying its best to improve the conditions of the village improve the conditions of the village and small scale industrial unit owners, still the sector as a show suffering from a few serious problems which are from a few serious problems which are discussed in the following paragraphs.

Financial: As discussed earlier the plan outlay for the programme of village and small scale industries has been inadequate in relation to its requirements. With the inclusion of more and more number of industries under the purview of village indust5iesw, there is a need for greater plan allocation in the future plans.

Keeping in view of the ever raising prices of the inputs required by the owners of the small scale industrial units, the total bank credit may be raised substantially (as against existing 30 per cent) for the development of village and small scale industrial units in India.

Raw Materials Adequate supply of raw materials on a sustained basis is a serious problem faced by these industries. There is pressing need for building up adequate supply of raw materials by the government agencies.

Technical Know-How: There has been rater slow in the process of development and application of appropriate technology in these industries. There is, thus, a phenomenal sickness in these industries. Hence, the necessary steps should be taken to adopt appropriate technology in village and small scale industries for better utilization of locally available resources including man-power in the country.

Prospects

It is admitted that the small scale industries is a vibrant sector which plays a vital row in the economic development of India. There is a lot of potential to be has harnessed. The prospects of this sector largely hinges on the provision of liberal finances both from financial intermediatories (commercial banks) and the Centre and the State Financial Corporations; reasonable rate of interest; marketing assistance through the Central and the State governments sales depots; regular supply of required quantity of raw materials at the nearest places of small scale industrial establishments; and institution based technical assistance and training programmes to periodically upgrade the skills and technical knowledge of the labours working in small scale industrial units.

To conclude, although the Government of India laid a considerable emphasis on the need to develop village and small scale industries in rural areas of the country. The percentage of financial allocation made for this sector in the successive five year plans do not reflect it adequately. This is corroborated with the facts presented in Table 11.1. The highest financial allocation for this sector was made available only in the Second/five Year Plan. It may be seen form the table that financial allocation for the development of village and small scale industries had fluctuated between 1.5 per cent to 2.8 per cent of the total plan outlay set for the plan period. And it is sickening to note that the Eighth five Year Plan draft makes a mention that only 1.32 per cent of the total public outlay would be made available for the development of village and small scale industries in the rural areas where more than 70 per cent of the country's population live. It is understood that this sector has accounted for contribution 10 per cent to the industrial output as such it would be desirable to raise the present investment level (allocation 10 per cent of the Public) for the growth and development of village and small scale industries in the country, in the plan that follows. The diversification of village and small scale industrial units coupled with their rapid rate of growth would effectively tackle the twin problems of unemployment and poverty in the country.

12

Role of Infrastructural Facilities in Sustainable Development of Tribal People

The tribals are the indigenous people of India who are generally called 'Adivasis' which literally means original setters. The constitution of India has a specified certain Scheduled Tribes (STs) to avail themselves of special treatment or specialties or privileges for their socio-economic development, as the STs for one of the most backward sections of our country. Through there has been a gradual increase in their literacy rates since independence, the present position is far from satisfactory (Mohanthy, P.K., 2003).

Tribes in Andhra Pradesh

As per the 1991 census there are more than 450 tribes in India. Out of which more than 33 are found in Andhra Pradesh.

Total population of A.P. is 6.65 crore (as per 1991 census). Out of which 41.9 lakh Scheduled Tribes accounting for 6.31 per cent to the total population in A.P. as against 8.08 per cent at the National level. They are mostly concentrated in hill areas over the State.

As per the 2001 census of Anantapur District in 35.68 lakh. Out of this the ST population is 1.25 lakh-comprising of 64,657 males and 60,605 females-and thus accounting for 3.5 per cent of the population in the district of Anantapur.

Education among Tribals in Anantapur District

Although Anantapur district is the most backward district in the state of A.P., the literacy levels attained in the district are quite satisfactory as per latest statistical figures 59 per cent among men and 37 per cent among females are literates in the district.

But in the case of Sts these figures are as that of 42 per cent among men and 15 among women are literates which call for quick remedial measures to tone up educational literacy levels among STs in the district.

Education is one of the important agents of social change. Most of the tribal communities are educationally very backward in the district. The Sts have no access to educational and other infrastructural facilities as most of them-more than 95 per cent of the tribals-levels either in hill areas or in inaccessible areas to safeguard their cultural identity. An attempt is made here to highlight the crucial role played by infrastructural facilities and community support in the improvement of tribal village called Naginaini Cheruvu Thanda in Somandepalli mandal of Anantpaur district.

Naginaini Cheruvu Thanda, with over 350 households comprising of 1200 population, with 660 males and 540 females, of Somandepalli Mandal, Anantapur district of A.P. stands as a distinct place for all-round development of ST community. Unlike other St Communities else where, the STs in Naginaini Cheruvu Thanda have not been eking out their livelihood from the forest based resources as there are no worth mentioning forest near habitant. That is to say, its only agriculture that sustains them.

Till late 1960's the people of this village were not exposed to the world outside their village and Somandepalli as they were engaged in agriculture and other allied activities. As population began to grow and agriculture failed to absorb additional man power; some able bodied youth say around 20-25 have entered into the department of the Indian Railways as gangmen in laying and maintaining railway tracks.

The gangmen who had secured jobs with regular stream of income started educating heir children, in addition to encouraging their tribe men to educate their children too. This has picked up the momentum resulted in surge towards education among the tribal community in the village.

Owing to conscious efforts made by the elderly trial men a handful of youth including women could get into government employment by 1975.

By 1985, it was reported that each tribal-house could have a minimum of one member working in government sector. It is rather heartening note that tribal men from this village have occupied prestigious positions such as judges-one of the judges of the Honorable A.P. High Court hails from this village and a few others as Judges in the lower courts of A.P-one Collector, one Deputy Collector, Lawers, Engineers, Teachers, Clerks, Office-in-Treasuries, Police Officers, Agricultural Extension Officers in university, Lecturers, Postal employees and an Executive Director of SC Corporation, Anantapur.

It is not only men who could get into Government jobs. A significant number of women from this village started to have been working as doctors, Treasury Officials, Teachers and in the Department of Revenue as Clerks and other cadres.

The field level experience is rewarding to know that each tribal household in the village on a minimum has one-person employed in government sector, 2 persons in 25 per cent of the households while 3 people working in 10 per cent of the households and remaining households have comfortably settled themselves in agriculture and allied activities with relatively fair income.

The very fast factor that contributed for the educational awareness among the STs is the regular stream of income that the gangmen could get in the Railway department. This enabled them not only to sustain to their families, but also to meet the educational expenditure of their wards which includes their daughters too.

Through their periodic visits to the village the educated employees sensitized their tribal men with regard to the various privileges of the Government of India to promote educational and development among the STs in the country. As stated earlier the village could product Judge of A.P. court who maintained a good rapport with the village and used to educate them to make use of the Government schemes for the development of STs. This played a pivotal role in influencing tribal population to promote education among the tribal children.

The elderly educated tribal men who have been working in the state have sufficiently educated their fellow beings in the village in respect of getting financial assistance through the institutions, such as, local nationalized Bank, Corporative Bank, Rural Bank-Ananta Grameena bank and primary land Development Bank both for farming and non-farming activities. They could get required finances at a relatively cheaper of interest compared to the interest rates charged by local money lenders who charge a minimum interest of 24 per cent per annum, whereas bank rate of interest never exceeded 12.5 per cent per annum.

Since the village is situated in the two major urban centres: one, Hindupur-A grade Municipality and its south at distance of 25 kms; and two Penukonda-a Revenue Sub-Divisional Headquarters at a distance of 10 kms., the village could get access to all modern infrastructural facilities, including Navodaya Residential Schools and colleges which enabled them to move fast on the track of development with higher educational levels and employment in various sectors of the Government.

The village has the advantage of getting good marketing facilities for its mulberry silk cocoons both at Hindupur and Ramanagar near Bangalore in Karnataka. The farmers have been engaged in Sericulture activities. It is learned that the farmers have realized that the sericulture activities. It is learned that the farmers have realized that the sericulture is the best suites cash crop for them in the context of drought and as such they have been practicing sericulture since 1975 for the simile reason that on an average they have been raising three crops per year and each crop fetches them an income in the range of Rs.10000-12000 per acre per crop. This income has kept them in good stead to withstand the adverse effects of drought which frequents thrice in a soon of five years in the District.

By virtue of being close to Mandal Headquarters, two major urban centers railway line and the National Highway No.7 the tribal men were drawn more towards civilized society than buy any extremist/terrorist ideologies and activities as observed elsewhere in the State: Peace prevailing the village reported to have richly contributed for their social and economic progress. It is pertinent to recall the State Governments commitment to wean away from the clutches of extremists/terrorist activities by of providing jobs like Home guards. Police Constables and other jobs (vide TV Telecast DD-8 by Mr. Mohan Kanda, Chief Secretary, Government of Andhra Pradesh dated November 4, 2004).

The village could accomplish all this because of the availability of the infrastructural facilities which were made available to the tribal men within a radius of 2-3 kms. This facilitated for the fast education and employment growth and development of this village. The success story of Naginaini Cheruvu Thanda as analysed above may help the policy making body in designing such infrastructural facilities that trigger fast education and employment position in other tribal localities in the State and the country.

References

C.P. Yadav Encyclopedia of SCs and STs, Anmole Publications.

Government of A.P. Records in the Office of Tribal Welfare, Anantapur.

Government of A.P. Statistical Abstracts.

Government of India Educational Statistics of SCS and STs, Ministry of HRD, Government of India, New Delhi.

Government of India India 2001-Publication Division, Ministry of Information Board Casting, Government of India, New Delhi.

13

Regional Disparities in Andhra Pradesh

It is everybody's knowledge that the nature is the mine of wealth which has been distributed unevenly; this has caused the concentration of some factors, say, climate, perennial rivers, thick forests, mines with variety of mineral deposits, nearness to coastal areas and energetic people who shoulder tough tasks to develop their countries in a given period is substantiated by citing example of the Japanese who miraculously rebuild their economy which was totally destroyed by bomb blasts in the World War II.

It is pertinent to state here that although the presence of economic factors is a necessary condition to trigger fast economic development the sufficient condition is the manpower that can exploit the existing or available economic resources to maximize production of goods and services which are required to heighten the economic welfare of the people. Here again it is maintained that Japan stands 1st in the world in the production of quality Iron and Steel in abundant quantity despite the fact that it does not posses Iron and Steel mines within itself.

The State of Bihar presents a contrast picture in this regard; although Bihar is a mineral rich State but yet remains to be one of the poorest States in India. It is, therefore, inferred from the above discussion that sociological factors precede economic factors in achieving fast rate of development.

Regional disparities that were existing at the time of formation of the State due to historical reasons have been narrowed down; especially, it is more true in the case of education as has been evidenced from the fact that the professional colleges have been judiciously established in an even basis in all the districts of Andhra Pradesh. But it is also equally true that disparities still persist, crying for immediate removal. The long period of 46 years after the State formation and vast resources available were not used properly for the balanced and speedy development of the State. It is emphasized here that the government must impress the people of backward areas of the North Andhra, the South Telangana and the Rayalaseema regions about its seriousness to remove the persisting disparities. The government has to set priority areas for each region/district and make financial and administrative arrangements to overcome regional disparities in the state, with the involvement of all political parties.

The recent history of Andhra Pradesh underscore the fact that emotional integration of the people culminated in the formation of separate State on November 1st, 1956. The solemnly made gentleman's agreement on the state formation and six point formula announced by the centre and after the state had witnessed two big agitations have been grossly violated, resulted in fierce struggle to attain a separate statehood for the Telangana region in Andhra Pradesh.

The recent economic reforms introduced in the country have allowed unhindered Liberalisation and indiscriminate Privatisation based on free market ideology going to further worsen the regional disparities within the state. As a sequel to globals capitalism, here in the state also people move to areas which are already developed as it would facilitate them to have an access to the requirements easily and quickly with less cost. Further it is also easy and less costly to market their products in such areas. This naturally results in development of areas which are already developed living behind vast tracks of undeveloped areas in the state, accentuating the existing regional disparities in the state. It is observed that Hyderabad city and its surroundings and Visakhapatnam, Vijayawada, Anakapalli and Tirupati areas have been attracting more and more industries apart from being the centre of educational institutions.

In order to reduce the disparities among the regions if not, totally remove them the following suggestions are advanced:

1. The first and foremost important factors in achieving balanced regional development are total literacy and elimination of

gender discrimination and other Social disparities at the earliest. As of now only 54.6 per cent of the total population of the state are literates. Women in the agriculture sector not getting wages on par with men. Women are discriminated as the owners of the property and in the decision making process. These are to be addressed immediately. The government has to sensitize people especially of the backward and disadvantaged sections of the society.

2. The government has to ensure that it is wedded to growth with social justice and balanced regional development in the context of new economic reforms-Liberalisation, Privatisation and Globalisation (LPG). For the LPG is a market led economy allowing gaint corporations emerge with the merger or take over of even big companies at the global level. This is the dominant trend and natural consequence of development of global capitalism. This phenomenon makes the richer more richer and the poorer more poorer. It is here that the government's intervention is sought to reduce further glaring disparities arising due to globalization trends.
3. The State government should announce and implement a separate package for speedy development of Irrigation in the North Coastal area, South Telangana region and Rayalaseema where more than 70 per cent of Irrigation has been sustained with the groundwater. Water in all these regions in the most scarcest developmental input. Hence drip Irrigation should be developed in all the three regions on war-footing effort along with accelerated watershed development.
4. The small scale and cottage industries have been contributing over to 35 per cent of GDP, 38 per cent foreign exchange earnings and have provided more than 70 per cent of industrial workers in the country. Keeping in view of the importance this sector enjoys the government may reexamine the existing package schemes to promote this sector uniformly in the regions. The government may welcome expert's views to revitalize the small scale sector to withstand the shocks from globalization trends. It is emphasized that the

governments may issue orders to banks and financial institutions to liberally extend financial assistance for the development of this sector as in the case of China.

5. The government has to complete the Irrigation projects for which foundation-stone (s) have been laid. Any delay in these results in heart burn among the farmers. For instance as Chief Ministers both Sri. N.T. Rama Rao and Sri N. Chandrababu Naidu have laid foundation stones, one after the other, to the Hundri-Neeva projects, which was never executed. The present C.M. Dr. Y.S. Rajasekhar Reddy has also recently laid a foundation stone for the same project. This clearly brings to light that the plight of the farmers was not seriously taken care of by the government.
6. The farmers are to be educated on the effective utilization of water management techniques so as to maximize returns from the available water resources. Farmers in all drought areas are to be dissuaded from paddy cultivation and in its place, they may be encouraged to raise green grass on large scale to develop dairy which is highly suitable and remunerative work for the farmers, as dairy development in these areas tend to equalize earnings on par with farmers in non-drought prone in the districts.
7. The governments should put a stop for the establishment of any short of newly proposed any short institutions in the already over-crowded cities like Hyderabad, Visakhapatnam, Tirupati, Kakinada and Guntur. On the other hand all the newly proposed institutions/offices are to be located in middle and lower grade towns or mandal headquarters. If this is carried on at governmental level, it certainly effectively combats to certain extent, regional disparities in the context of development.
8. The Rayalaseema region enjoys relative disadvantage with respect to development of milk and dairy products, poultry and piggery, sheep and goat raring, cultivation of vegetables, fruits and flowers. The government may provide institutional and administrative assistance for the speedy development of

these sectors as it not only checks and rural exodus but also develop the region through income and employment generation within the region. This could be made possible with the joint cooperation of the government and the banking sector.

9. Review of the existing incentive package schemes in the context of globalization to achieve balanced regional development, such as, power-subsidy, free factory site and Tax concessions incentives to markets, goods, across national boundaries. The new package may be such as to accelerate the pace of development.
10. The F.D.I. provision may readily accepted provided if it helps to reduce regional disparities in the state.
11. It should be made mandatory that the M.P.LADS funds are to be spent only in the improvement of remote and backward areas.
12. The governments-the union and the State governments should discourage rapid urbanization of the already well developed cities and simultaneously initiated steps to fast promote urbanization in the medium and lower grade towns since it accelerates the pace of development with strong forward and backward linkages.
13. The Government should design such schemes which would exploit human resources to the maximum point when natural resources endowment is not paving a way for economic development. This fact is illustrated with the example: Anantapur, the most backward district in the country, has been endowed with manpower that can take up works that demand high skills and hard labour. Here the labour community, both in the formal and the non-formal sector not getting work for more than 5-6 months in a year. The Governments that are providing uniforms to Police, Home guards, Industrial works on site and in mines, military, Navy, Air Force, can get the uniform stitched in Anantapur district and thus provide jobs to thousands of tailors, similarly, the state government may think of establishing government

printing presses, stationary manufacturing units in backward district like Anantapur in Rayalaseema and provide employment on a sustainable basis.

14. Indiscriminate creation of Special Economic Zones (SEZs) within the state may further widen the gap between forward regions and backward regions within the state. It is therefore urged that the policy making body may take note of this fact.

As a matter of fact a few backward pockets could be or can be found even among the well developed nations of the world. For instance in a country like USA. There was one region called Tennessee Valley Project (TVP) which was identified as the most backward region/pocket in the country. It was the Roosevelt's government (1901-09) that flooded the region with government's simultaneous investments in multi sectors that catapulted Tennessee Valley to the status of highly developed one in a short period of time. Hence, it boils downs to state that the removal of regional disparities is, vastly, a matter of political choice. Disparities will progressively be erased if the government(s) committed to do so. It is well-nigh impossible to achieve balance regional development without a strong and committed political-will as is evidenced in the case of Tennessee valley project in USA.

References

Census of A.P. Economic Tables, Several Issues.

Dholakia, R.H. Regional Disparity in Economic Growth in India, Himalaya Publishing House, Bombay, 1985.

Five Year Plans Andhra Pradesh Statistical Abstract, 2001.

Myrdal, G. Economic theory and Underdeveloped Regions Methuen, London, 1957.

Myrdal, Gunnar Economic Theory and Under Developed Regions, Methuen, London.

North, D.C. Location and Regional economic Growth, Journal of Political Economy, June1955, p.243-58.

Rucghardson, H.W. Elements of Regional Economics, Penguine Books, Harmondsworth, 1960.

Sharma, J.V.M and Fiscal Imbalances in Andhra Pradesh, Asian Sreedevi Economic Review, Vol. XXXVI, No. 2, August 1999.

Williamson, J.G. Regional Inequality and the process of National Development: A Description of the patterns, Economic Development and Cultural Change, Vol.13, No.1, 1965.

14

Inter-regional Disparities in Infrastructure in Andhra Pradesh

Introduction

All those services that are required to create a modern economy are together addressed as infrastructure. These services have a wide range, from the provision of health services and education facilities to the supply of such needs as power, irrigation, transport, telecommunication, etc. Infrastructure has a two-way relationship with economic growth. One, infrastructure provides economic growth, and two; economic growth brings about changes in infrastructure. Infrastructure plays a pivotal role in the present days of Liberalisation, Privatisation Globalisation (LPG). As such infrastructure is likened to arterial system in the human body. According to the World Bank Report 1994, infrastructure represents the wheel of economic activity if not the engine. It is understood that there exists a strong association between Infrastructure and Economic development.

It is pertinent to recall V.K.R.V. Rao's comment while analyzing the importance of infrastructure: "this function of infrastructure is to release latent productivity in the factors of production singly and in coordination and bring about not only an increase in the output of individual factors and units of production but also mutually additive effect through cooperation in inputs, outputs and space and time and thus maximize the overall rate of economic growth".

The growth in GDP is directly proportional to the degree of infrastructure made available in a country. There is considerable consensus that improvements in infrastructure will have a strong impact upon GDP growth and poverty alleviation. The pace of economic growth attained by a country is solely depending upon strong infrastructural base.

No nation can build the structure of the social and economic well-being of its people on weak foundation. A well conceived and well-built social and economic infrastructure not only brings speed in economic growth but also marks proper utilization of potentialities of natural resources, human-resources, water-resources, agro-based resources etc. Everyone requires good hospitals, properly staffed by doctors and paramedical staff, schools and colleges with libraries, laboratories and sports facilities for the all-round personality development of growing children. And these medical or educational centres must be within easy reach. And that focus on the importance of communications at the local, state, national and international levels. We always talk about the global village and global connectivity. Good roads, highways, bridge, railway lines, airports, seaports, telecommunication, twenty-four hour uninterrupted power supply these are no longer luxury items, but a basic necessity in today's world. India is a nation on the move and in a highly competitive and globalised society. Its progress may hamper if it does not build a proper social and economic infrastructure.

This article analyses the trends in infrastructure in India and Andhra Pradesh in the process of 'Economic Development' during the post reforms period i.e., 1991 to 2001-02. To say more specifically an attempt is made to study the levels of Infrastructure Development in Andhra Pradesh vis-à-vis the all India level during the period under reference-post reforms period.

Early, during the Vajpayee regime a Task Force (TF) on infrastructure was constituted to attract investments in specific projects of national and regional importance and ensure their timely completion. The terms of reference of the Task-Force included the determination of the routes for expressways and national highways and establish technical parameters. The Task Force is also entrusted with the task of identifying and recommending locations of airports along with establishing benchmarks and criteria for airports. It also lays down criteria for competitive bidding and selection of Engineering Procurement and Construction (EPC) contractors. It also oversees and monitors timely implementation of the projects. For these reasons, the thrust of infrastructure policy has been to create a sound regulatory framework. Private firms would operate in this regulatory environment, and produce infrastructure services. The role for regulation is to protect the interest of consumers, obtain conditions of competition, and farther the institutional framework. In areas like rural infrastructure, where cost recovery is innately difficult, there is a greater role for government to foster infrastructure provision even if it is not directly profitable.

The ultimate goal of infrastructure policy is to effectively deliver infrastructure services of high quality and at low price, to households and firms in the country. The success of policies in infrastructure must be judged by the quality, quantity and prices that end users are charged for these services, and comparisons with global standards on each of these three fronts.

Nature of Infrastructure

The infrastructure sector has certain peculiarities that help us to distinguish this sector from other sectors of the economy. Among these, the more important distinguishing features can be identified as follows:

- **Public Goods:** Most of the physical infrastructure services have some elements of public good in them. These services are available to the public; the consumers may be charged for these services or the same may be supplied free. But even when they are supplied against a price, it is not always possible to exclude those consumers who chose not to pay for them.
- **Externalities:** The social benefit of the infrastructure services far exceeds the cost involved in their generation. This in turn creates problems in pricing of these services. It makes it difficult to price them in order to recover the cost fully.
- **Monopolies:** Due to the inherent nature of infrastructure services, it is difficult for more than one supplier to exist in one location. It thus creates the possibility for monopolies

and their regulation.

- **Public Sector Domination:** The existence of externalities particularly in the field of social welfare has resulted in a dominant position by public sector in production and supply of infrastructure services.

Infrastructure and Economic Growth

Infrastructure has a two-way relationship with economic growth. One, infrastructure promotes economic growth, and two, economic growth brings about changes in infrastructure.

- Output of infrastructure sector such as power, water, transport, etc., are used as inputs for production in the directly productive sectors (manufacturing, agriculture etc.). Therefore, insufficient availability of the former may result in sub-optimal utilization of assets in the latter.
- Infrastructure developments such as transport improve productivity significantly.
- Infrastructure provides key to modern technology in practically all sectors.
- A close association has been observed between infrastructure spending on the one hand and GDP growth on the other. Studies have indicated that 1 per cent growth in the infrastructure stock is associated with 1 per cent growth in per capita GDP.
- Generally around 6.5 per cent of the total value added is contributed by infrastructure services in low income countries. This proportion increases to 9 per cent in middle income countries and 11 per cent in high income countries.
- Given the above type of linkage, infrastructural development is important not only for economic growth, globalization and technological innovation in manufacturing but also for poverty reduction.

Trends in Infrastructure Sector

In 2004-05, the infrastructure sector experienced mixed outcomes. The growth rate in some key sectors showed acceleration from the previous year. In particular, strong growth rates have been observed for electricity, railways, ports and civil aviation.

1. Hydel generation showed a sharp turnaround, reflecting the good monsoon, from a 13.8 per cent decline in 2002-03 to a 15.6 per cent increase in 2003-04. It continued to enjoy high growth in the year 2004-05, showing 17.6 per cent growth rate. It showed a change over of 5.1 in 2004-05 as compared to 4.1 in 2003-04, while nuclear generation growth showed negative growth -8.3 and -7.2 in year 2003-04 and 2004-05 respectively.
2. The goods traffic carried by the railways showed a strong acceleration from 5.3 per cent growth in 2002-03 to 7.7 per cent growth in 2004-05. The cargo handled at major ports also grew by 11.1 per cent in 2004-05, as compared with 9 per cent in 2002-03.
3. The telecom sector continued to progress by maintaining the high growth rates observed since 2000 onwards. But it showed a declining growth rate (21.4 per cent) in April December 2004-05 as compared to 29.1 per cent in 2003-04 for the same period.
4. In the area of civil aviation, domestic passenger traffic grew sharply by 25.9 per cent in 2004-05, as compared with a 10.4 per cent growth in the previous year.

Infrastructure Development during the Plan Period

As can be seen that the size of our plans has been increasing. The First Five Year Plan was relatively smaller plan with a total expenditure of Rs.1,960 crore. This has increased in the X Plan to projected outlay of Rs. 15,25,639 crore. As is clear from the Table 14.1 agriculture was given top priority during the I and IV plans while industry was accorded top priority in the II and V Plans. Because of these priorities the VI Plan brought to light the growing significance of power sector in the economy. The power sector became a crucial sector because of (a) growing needs of power in industry and agriculture, and (b) sharp rise in the prices

Table 14.1: Sectoral Distribution of the Public Sector Expenditure (Percentage)

Sector/Plan	I	II	III	Annual	IV	V	VI	VII	VIII	IX	X
Agriculture	37.0	20.9	20.6	23.8	23.3	20.5	25.4	21.8	22.10	22.70	18.7
Power	7.6	9.7	14.6	18.3	18.6	17.8	27.2	30.4	26.60	25.40	26.5
Industry	4.9	24.1	23.9	24.7	19.7	26.0	15.4	13.3	10.80	8.20	10.7
Transport & Communications	26.4	22.0	24.6	18.5	19.5	17.5	15.9	16.3	18.70	19.80	21.3
Social Services	24.1	23.3	16.3	14.7	18.9	18.2	16.1	18.2	21.80	23.90	22.8
Total	100	100	100	100	100	100	100	100	100	100	100

Source: Five Year Plan Documents, Government of India.

of Crude oil created foreign exchange difficulties for India. Hence there was a need to acquire self reliance in the power sector. One can observe that there was a significant increase in the plan outlay for power sector in the VII Five Year Plan onwards and it was up to the X Five Year Plan. The plan outlay for power sector was 17.8 per cent in the V plan while it was 27.2 per cent in the VI plan further it went up to 30.4 per cent in the VII plan; thereafter it slightly declined to 26 per cent in the succeeding plans. It is because of the fact that the private sector vigorously participated in power generation and marketing of the same.

During the I Plan more than 58 per cent (Power, Transport & Communication and Social Sectors) of the plan outlay was allotted to infrastructure sector which went up to 70.6 per cent during the X Five Year Plan showing the concern bestowed by the government for the improvement of the vital sector of the infrastructure.

Trends in Infrastructure in the Post Reforms Period

The facts presented in Table 14.2 shows that coal production was almost doubled between 1997-98 and 2004-05. Electricity generated declined rather sharply between 2000-01 and 2003-04 and it almost regained its earliest pace in 2004-05. Here it may be mentioned that Hydel Power started picking up its momentum from 2003-04.

There were wide fluctuations in the production of Steel and Cement during the period under discussion. Railways provided a good network for the transport of goods which resulted in the good Revenue earning through goods traffic.

The spectacular achievement was recorded in the telecommunication sector during all through the post reform period. The Export Cargo sector was subjected to ups and downs between 2000-01 to 2004-05 while Import of Cargo handled showed positive trend from 2002-03 onwards.

In order to draw a comparative picture in respect of the levels of infrastructure development in the State of Andhra Pradesh and

Table 14.2: Trends in Growth Rate of Infrastructure Sectors (Per cent)

Item	Unit	1997-98	1998-99	1999-2000	2000-01	2001-02	2002-03	2003-04	2004-05
I. Energy									
1. Coal Production	Mn. tonnes	3.6	-2.5	3.1	3.5	4.2	4.6	3.9	6.8
2. Electricity generated (Utilities only)	Bn. Kwh	6.6	6.6	7.2	3.9	3.1	3.2	3.4	6.5
(a) Hydel	"	8.5	11.0	-2.5	-7.6	-0.7	-13.7	10.5	17.5
(b)Thermal (incl, nuclear)	"	6.2	5.7	9.3	7.4	2.5	6.2	2.4	4.7
3. Petrolium									
(a) Crude oil production	Mn. tonnes	3.0	-3.4	-2.4	1.5	-1.2	3.2	-0.5	2.9
(b) Refinery throughput	Mn. tonnes	3.7	5.2	25.4	20.3	3.7	4.9	7.2	6.7
II Steel	Mn. tonnes	6.3	1.4	15.0	6.4	3.6	10.1	12.2	3.8
III Cement	Mn. tonnes	9.1	5.7	14.2	-0.9	7.4	8.8	5.6	6.9

Contd…

Weighted Average growth I to III		5.7	2.8	9.1	5.1	3.2	5.6	5.8	5.4
IV Transport and Communications									
1. Railway revenue-earning Goods traffic	Mn. tonnes	5.0	-2.0	8.4	3.7	4.0	5.3	7.0	7.7
2. Cargo handled at major ports	Mn. tonnes	10.7	0.0	8.0	3.4	2.3	9.0	7.5	11.1
3. Telecommunications	000 Nos.	27.1	16.4	29.7	27.2	23.9	21.5	29.1	21.4
4. Civil Aviation									
a) Export cargo handled	000 tonnes	6.2	-3.9	10.3	5.1	4.1	13.3	0.0	11.8
b) Import cargo handled	000 tonnes	-5.9	-0.5	15.4	3.6	-1.0	18.6	9.7	30.1
c) Passenger handled at International Terminals	Mn.	4.6	1.0	2.9	4.6	-5.0	4.8	4.7	15.7
d) Passenger handled at Domestic Terminals	Mn.	-1.8	0.9	6.9	7.7	-5.7	9.6	10.4	25.9

Sources: Item No.I to III Ministry of Commerce & Industry, IV. I Ministry of Railways, IV. 2 and 4 Ministry of Statistics and Programme Implementation and IV. 3 Ministry of Communication.

all India level, it is felt desirable to make a break-up analysis of economic infrastructure and social infrastructure.

The data relating to the selected indicators of infrastructure development of Andhra Pradesh and India for the period 1990-91 to 2001-02 are show in Table 14.3.

As can be seen from the table, per capita domestic power consumption (in kwh) of Andhra Pradesh has increased from 28.03 in 1990-91 to 37.79 by 2002-03 while the all India average decreased from 74.23 to 68.80 during the period. The percentage consumption of Electricity in Agriculture (in cro. kwh) in total production has decreased from 0.66 in 1990-91 to 0.02 by 2002-03 while at the All India level, it decreased from 3.33 to 1.89 during the same period. The Electric pump sets per 10,000 hectares of net irrigated area is an important factor in rural infrastructure. In Andhra Pradesh there is remarkable increase in the application of electric pump sets. The electric pump sets per 10,000 hectares of net irrigated area has increased from 3,495.87 is in 1990-91 to 6,478.01 in 2002-03 while that of the nation increased from 2,150.50 to 2,868.10 during the period.

On the transport sector, the percentage of surfaced road length to total road length of Andhra Pradesh has increased from 46.80 kms. In 1990-91 to 57.34 kms., by 2002-03 while the road length per 1000 sq. km. of area has increased from 54.2 kms. to 62.2 kms., during the same period. The all India averages have also shows an increased in both these indicators. The Railway route length per 1000 sq. kms. of area has increased marginally from 18.4 kms in 1990-91 to 18.89 by 2002-03 in the state, while the country's average increased from 20.1 kms. to 21.22 kms., during the same period. The number of registered vehicles per lakh of population has been doubled from 2192 to 4395 during the same period in the state. The country's average has also recorded in impressive jump in this regard.

On the communication front, it is disheartening to note that the number of post offices per 100 sq. Kms. has decreased from 6.00 in 1990-91 to 5.88 in 2002-03. Similarly the long distance public telephone call offices per lakh of population have also

Table 14.3: Infrastructure Development in India and Andhra Pradesh

No.		1990-91 Andhra Pradesh	All India	2002-03 Andhra Pradesh	All India
Economic Infrastructure:					
A	**Power**				
1.	Per Capita Domestic Consumption in kwH	28.03	37.79	74.23	68.80
2.	Per cent as to consumption of electricity in agriculture	0.66	0.02	3.33	1.89
3.	No. of electric pump sets per 10,000 hectares of NIA	3495.87	2150.50	6478.01	2868.10
B	**Transport**				
4.	Percentage of surfaced road length to total road length	46.80	55.19	57.34	61.41
5.	Road length per 1000 sq. km. of area	54.20	65.30	62.20	76.80
6.	Railway route length per 1000 sq. km. of area	18.40	20.10	18.89	21.22
7.	Registered vehicles per lakh of population	2192.20	2783.00	4395.00	4531.00
C	**Communications**				
8.	No. of post offices per 100 sq. km.	6.00	4.52	5.88	4.72
9.	Long Distance Public Telephone Call Offices per lakh population	2.44	1.96	2.00	1.30
10.	No. of telegraph offices per 100 sq. km.	0.90	'2.50	10.41	27.06

Contd...

D	**Banks**				
11.	No. of commercial banks per lakh of population	13.91	13.65	14.52	15.43
12.	No. of branches of cooperative societies per lakh of population	6.97	43.80	73.84	50.65
13.	No. of branches of Regional Rural Bank population	1.69	1.71	1.53	1.40
Social Infrastructure:					
A	**Education**				
14.	No. of Primary Schools per lakh of population	73.90	66.27	64.57	58.77
15.	No. of Upper Primary Schools per lakh of population	10.30	1.03	10.21	17.55
16.	No. of High Schools per lakh of population	10.95	0.52	10.91	9.75
17.	No. of vocational Schools per lakh of population	0.34	0.15	2.89	0.21
B	**Health**				
18.	No. of allopathic hospitals and dispensaries per lakh of population	27.37	4.67	2.67	3.91
19.	No. of beds (all types) per lakh of population	46.62	72.52	46.14	69.41
20.	No. of doctors available per lakh of population	10.03	46.50	11.37	56.74

Source: (i) Statistical Abstract of India – 1991, 2003; (ii) Census of India: 1991 & 2001; (iii) Economic Survey of India, 1991, 2001 & 2005.

decreased from 2.44 to 2.00 during the same period in the state. However, there is an increase in number of telephone exchanges per 100 sq, kms. During 1990-91 from 0.73 to 1.14 by 2002-03 in the Andhra Pradesh while the national averages has increased from 0.36 in 1990-91 to 25.37 by 2002-03. The number of telegraph offices per 100 sq. kms., has also increased phenomenally both at the state and All India level.

The number of commercial banks per lakh of population has increased from 13.91 in 1990-91 to 14.52 by 2002-03, while the nation average has increased from 13.65 to 15.43 during the same period. The number of cooperative society branches per lakh of population has increased phenomenally from 6.97 in 1990-91 to 73.84 by 2002-03 in the state of Andhra Pradesh, while the nation average increased from 43.80 to 50.65 during the same period. It is however, disheartening to note that the number of Regional Rural Bank Branches per lakh of population has decreased from 1.69 in 1990-91 to 1.53 by 2002-03 at the state level while the nation average has also registered a decline from 1.71 to 1.40 during the same period. The analysis of economic infrastructure thus revealed a rosy picture in respect of the most of the indicators grouped under economic infrastructure during the same period under study and also in comparison to the All India level.

In respect of social infrastructure, an exercise is made to study the education levels and health status in the state of Andhra Pradesh vis-à-vis All India level. On education front, it is disheartening to note that the number of primary schools per lakh of population in Andhra Pradesh has decreased from 73.90 in 1990-91 to 64.57 by 2002-03 while the nation average also decreased from 66.27 to 58.77 during the same period. The number of upper primary schools per lakh of population in Andhra Pradesh has also decreased from 10.30 in 1990-91 to 10.21 in 2002-03 while the country average has increased impressively from a mere 1.03 to 17.55 during the same period. The number of high schools per lakh of population in Andhra Pradesh has also decreased marginally from 10.95 in 1990-91 to 10.91 in 2002-03 but at the All India level the average has jumped from 0.52 to 9.75 during the same period. However, the number of vocational institutions per lakh of population has increased impressively from 0.34 to 2.89 during the same period in the state while All India level average has also recorded an impressive jump. It is also disheartening to note that the number of allopathic hospitals and dispensaries available per lakh of population in the Andhra Pradesh has decreased from 27.37 in 1990-91 to 26.7 by 2002-03, while the All India average has also decreased from 4.67 to 3.91 during the same period.

Similarly, the number of beds available per lakh of population has also decreased marginally from 46.62 to 46.14 during the same period. However, the most refreshing feature in that there is an increase in the number of doctors available per lakh of population during 1990-91 from 10.03 to 11.37 in the state of Andhra Pradesh, while national averages also registered an increase from 46.50 to 56.74 during the same period.

Status of Irrigational facilities in Rayalaseema Region

The status of irrigation facilities in Rayalaseema region between 1994-95 and 2001-02 is presented in Table 14.4. The gross area irrigated in Rayalaseema in 2001-02 is less than 7.89 per cent of its geographical area while it is 21.00 per cent in Telangana and 27.37 per cent in Coastal Andhra region. Area irrigated more than once in Rayalaseema region is 1.52 per cent of its geographical area as against 5.04 per cent in Telangana and 7.07 per cent in Coastal Andhra region in 2001-02. This shows that the irrigational facilities in Rayalaseema have been very limited the efforts of the government to expand the area under different sources of irrigation did not yield positive results.

An enquiry into the area irrigated under different sources in Rayalaseema reveals interesting facts. Net area irrigated under canals in Rayalaseema declined from 22.90 per cent in 1994-95 to 17.45 per cent in 2001-02. On the other hand the percentage of net area irrigated under tube wells increased significantly from 22.71 to 41.58 during 1994-2002. This is dangerous and adversely affects the ecological balance of the region where ground water

Table: 14.4 Inter-regional Disparities in Infrastructural Facilities in Andhra Pradesh

S. No.	Details	Coastal Andhra		Telangana		Rayalaseema	
		1993-94	2001-02	1993-94	2001-02	1993-94	2001-02
1.	No. of hospitals & dispensaries (in per cent)	42.38	42.12	38.23	38.22	19.37	19.64
2.	Number of beds (in per cent)	38.18	37.08	44.77	45.93	17.03	16.98
3.	Number of doctors (in per cent)	39.30	39.02	42.95	40.75	17.74	20.21
4.	No. of motor vehicles APSRTC (in per cent)	37.61	36.63	42.66	43.03	19.72	20.32
5.	No. of motor vehicles private (in per cent)	48.92	51.84	14.20	12.30	36.87	35.85
6.	No. of post-offices (in per cent)	41.03	41.05	36.22	36.19	22.75	22.74
7.	No. of telephone exchanges (in per cent)	40.23	40.02	36.75	39.36	23.01	20.61
8.	No. of bank offices	2101	2296	1900	2178	777	848
9.	Population per bank office	14000	14444	15000	15400	16000	16250
10.	Black top road length (PR) Kms	3374	4587	1057	5729	569	1689
11.	Road length per 000 Sq.km (in km)	0.36	0.49	0.60	0.59	0.04	0.25

Contd...

12.	Net area irrigated	21.75	20.77	12.60	15.24	5.24	6.37
13.	Percentage to geographical area	23.50	22.44	11.01	13.31	7.80	9.47
14.	Net area irrigated under canals (in per cent)	57.66	57.77	18.33	16.17	22.90	17.45
15.	Net area irrigated under Tanks (in per cent)	19.21	14.25	17.30	12.58	10.50	12.24
16.	Net area irrigated under Tube wells & other wells (in per cent)	18.02	22.24	17.15	67.21	64.50	68.13
17.	Net area irrigated under other sources (in per cent)	5.06	5.54	4.69	3.39	1.19	2.04

Source: Directorate of Economics & Statistics, Govt. of A.P., Statistical Abstracts of Andhra Pradesh, 2003, Hyderabad.

level is receding fast making the lives of the people miserable. Governmental policy to provide loans and subsidy to deepening of the old wells and sinking of new wells in this drought prone area resulted in sinking of tube wells for irrigation and contributed to the depletion of ground water level in the region. Perhaps, this is the reason for the increase in the gross area irrigated and net area irrigated in Rayalaseema region during 1994-2003. Infact, well irrigation in drought prone areas is a luxury and sinking of tube wells is to be discouraged firmly.

Status of Infrastructural Facilities in Rayalaseema Region

The details relating to some of the Infrastructural facilities available in Rayalaseema region during 1994-2002 are shown in Table 14.4. The number of hospitals showed in increasing trend and their number per 000 population has been 3 in all the three regions during 1994-2002. Number of beds per 000 population remained constant in Coastal Andhra region and declined in the other two regions during this period. However, the rate of decline in Rayalaseema is more than that of Telangana region. The number of doctors per 000 population increased in Coastal Andhra and Rayalaseema regions and remained unchanged in Telangana region. All this indicates that there is no significant improvement in the medical facilities provided in Rayalaseema region.

The number of APSRTC motor vehicles on road showed an increasing trend in all the regions during 1994-2002. But, motor vehicles per 000 population remained unchanged in all the three regions. The number of private motor vehicles on road increased in Coastal Andhra region while it declined in other two regions. Private motor vehicles per 000 population in Rayalaseema region decreased while it remained constant in other two regions during the period under review. Though, the length of black top roads (Panchayat Raj) increased significantly in all the three regions, road length per 000 sq. kms. has been very low in Rayalaseema and in fact it has been less than one half of the road length in other two regions. This shows that there is no improvement in the transport facilities provided by the government in Rayalaseema region.

The number of post offices serving 000 population declined in all the three regions during the period under review. This is perhaps, due to the expansion of private courier services. There is no change in the number of telephone exchanges serving 000 population is 4 in all the three regions of the state. Though, there has been a rise in the number of bank offices, the average population per bank office also increased in all the three regions. However, the rise in the number of population on each bank is more in Rayalaseema region compared to other two regions. From this it is clear that the Infrastructural facilities provided in Rayalaseema region have been highly inadequate.

Conclusion

The review of infrastructure development in India reveals hard facts: rural areas are have stagnated atmosphere and their relative position remained unchanged from 1960 to 2006. This is a gross negligence of 70 per cent of the people that live in rural areas; on the other hand the urban centres where less than 30 per cent of the people live have all the good infrastructure. This urban-biased economy does not augur well in the context of globalization. Rural transport system needs to be strengthened with all-whether roads with adequate number of vehicles to facilitate rural people, more so farmers who frequent up on urban centres for the sale of Agriculture Product. It is a common site to observe farmers often sit with their agricultural produce on the top of the bus on his way to market. Farmers have been facing a lot of problems due to transport bottlenecks. This has seriously come in the way of rural development.

It is, therefore, felt that the private sector may be encouraged to take the necessary initiative to provide the needed basic infrastructure in the rural areas which triggers the fast rate of economic growth in the country. For a major constraint on growth has been infrastructure, particularly power, roads, ports, and communications and the higher outlays in the current budget

(2006-07) on these areas are a welcome feature.

Thus, the analysis of Social infrastructure in the State of Andhra Pradesh during the study period revealed that the Rayalaseema is lagging behind in infrastructural development vis-à-vis the other two regions in the state. However, the only exception in this regard, is the number of doctors available per lakh of population, showed a positive improvement.

References

G.O.I., "INDIA 2005- A REFERENCE ANNUAL", Research, Reference and Training Division, director, Publications Division, Ministry of Information & Broadcasting, Government of India, Patiala House, new Delhi – 110001.

G.O.I., Economic Survey of India 2004-05, Ministry of Finance.

Sapna N. Singh, Yojana, A Development Monthly, Republic Day Special, January 2005,Vol. 49, Yojana Bhavan, Sansad Marg, New Delhi.

Sapna N. Singh, Yojana, A Development Monthly, Vol.49, May 2005, Yojana Bhavan, Sansad Marg, New Delhi.

The Hindu, "The Hindu", Editorial Page, Wednesday, March 1st, 2006, Bangalore, P10.

V.K.R.V. Rao, "Investment Income and multiplier in an underdeveloped Economies in agriculture", A.N. Singh, S.P. (eds), The Economics of Underdevelopment, Oxford University Press, Bombay, 1958, p.9.

Part III: Natural Resources and Environmental Protection

By
G. Satyanarayana
M. Reddi Ramu
Y. Kesava Reddy
M.V. Raghavulu

15

Air Pollution and its Impact on Environment

Introduction

The word 'Pollution' has its origin in Latin: 'Polluere' which means contaminate any aspect of nature or environment. Pollution is defined as contamination of the environment in such a way that it creates hazards or potential hazards to the health, safety and welfare of the living and non-living species. Pollution takes place when dirty or harmful substances combine with air, water, land etc., so that it is no longer pleasant to use them.

India's environmental problems are mainly due to its high population presence and limited natural resources India accounts for 15 per cent of the world's population but has only 2.4 per cent of the world's land area. Our development process has not only ignored environmental consideration but has been an unjust and imbalanced development. Our natural resources are getting depleted at alarming rates. Some 1.5 million hectares of land, turn barren every year because of deforestation.

According to the report of the National Commission on Floods (1980) the annual expenditure on flood and drought relief is more than Rs. 1,500 crore which is in addition to the colossal loss of life and property. In India, every year 2.5 million hectares of land turns into waste land due to environmental degradation. Besides these, Industrial activities, Motor transport and burning of fossil fuels have been emitting large quantities of pollutants into the atmosphere. Even rivers are also polluted by untreated effluents from industries reducing the availability of drinking water. All these are the environment problems existing in India.

Need for Good Environment

Environment is defined as physical and biological

surroundings of a living being. All living beings require certain conditions for their sustained living; for this the environs in which they live matter much.

The Government of India took initiative appropriate laws in order to provide safe environmental conditions.

The government has recognized the need for land and water resources management and the protection of environmental resources to be included in the constitution since 1977. The constitution (42nd Amendment) Act of 1977 obligates the Government to protect and improve environment for the good of the society as a whole.

India's first national law on environment was the insecticides Act enacted in 1968 for regulating the import, manufacture, sale, transport, distribution and use of insecticides in order to reduce harm to human beings or animals. The Act however, did not provide for any compensation or damages arising out of poisoning from insecticides and failed to check the growth of misbranded and spurious products.

The year 1972 was a land mark in the history of environmental management in India. India in this particular year attempted the first national efforts to address environmental protection through the formation of the National Committee of Environmental Planning and Co-ordination. The NCEPC was setup in 1972 to prepare reports on the state of environment in India for the Human Environment Conference at Stockholm in June 1972. It was setup to promote greater co-ordination and integration in environmental policies and programmes. This Committee was mandated to advise the government on environment problems and assess environmental consequences of large development projects.

In the same year (1962) the Wild Life Protection Act was enacted to provide the protection of wild animals and birds. The act provided the constitution of a Wild Life Advisory Board for each state regulation of the hunting of wild animals and birds and specified procedures for declaring areas as sanctuaries and national parks.

The first National law for air pollution control was enacted in 1974. The Water (prevention and control of pollution) Act of 1974 marked an important milestone in environment legislation in India.

What is Air Pollution?

Air is found everywhere. Air may get polluted by natural causes, for example, volcanic activity, which releases ash, dust and sulphur compounds; forest or grass fires caused by lightning; or by man-made causes such as industrial and vehicular emissions.

Sources of Air Pollution: Air pollution consists of gases, liquids or solids present in the atmosphere in high enough levels to harm humans, other organisms or materials.

Pollutants in the air may be in the form of solid particles or gases. The solid particles that remained suspended in the air are called suspended particulates. They may reduce visibility or damage human health. Air can also be polluted by trace metals such as lead, nickel, iron, zinc and copper. There are several types of gaseous pollutants which have different impacts on human health and the environment.

Air pollutants are often divided into two categories: Primary and Secondary. Primary air pollutants are emitted or discharged from the source directly into the atmosphere, such as sulphur dioxide and nitrogen oxides from the burning of coal in thermal power plants. Secondary air pollutants are the products of chemical reactions involving primary air pollutants. For example, as the emissions from coal-based power plants are carried away by winds, chemical reactions take place which convert the emissions into secondary pollutants – nitrogen dioxide, nitric acid vapour, and droplets containing sulphuric acid, sulfate and nitrate salts. The acidic chemicals come down to the earth's surface as acid rain.

The sources and effects of air pollution are varied and complex. Some sources of man-made air pollution are vehicular emissions, industrial processes and the burning of fuels in homes.

Indoor air pollution is one of the largest health risk factors in the world. Research shows that about 6 per cent of all deaths each year result from breathing elevated levels of indoor smoke from biomass fuels. Over 80 per cent of the people in the rural areas of India rely mainly on solid biomass fuels for cooking and heating. This produces large amounts of smoke and other air pollutants in the confined space of the home, resulting in high exposures.

There are more than 7,50,000 man-made chemicals present in our environment and to this 1,000-2,000 new ones are added every year. And, all the pollutants put together 2 billion tons of air pollutants are released every year. On a global scale 2,900 Million Tons Per Annum (MTPA) of particulates, 480 MTPA of NO_X, 10^6 MTPA of CO_2, 3800 MTPA of CO, 260 MTPA of SO_X, 4 MTPA of H_2S, 5300 MTPA of ammonia and 1600 MPTA of hydrocarbons are released. The sources of the four main pollutants for air pollution are mentioned in Table 15.1.

Table 15.1: Sources of Air Pollution (%)

Pollutant	Industries	Combustion	Solid waste	Transportation
SPM	30	30	20	20
SO_2	15	80	NIL	5
NO_X	4	48	NIL	48
CO	7	20	7	66

Source: Air Pollution and Control, Kaushal & Co., 51-10-10, Sattemmagudi Street, Jagannaickpur, Kakinada.

Man can survive for 5 weeks without food, 5 days without water and less than 5 minutes without air. This is attributed to the fact that he breathes, on an average, 25,000 times a day at a rate of 1-2 liters of air per breath. Compared to the consumption of drinking water of about 2 liters a day (2 kg/day) man consumes about 20,000 times more of air by volume and 25 times more by weight. Thus man requires enormous quantities of air for his survival. In addition, the air he breathes goes into direct contact with the most sensitive organs of the human body-the respiratory tract and the lungs. Thus the quality of air he breathes has a direct bearing on his health and well being. Unfortunately, man is not equipped with household or portable air cleaning devices unlike water filters etc. and thus demands a clean ambient air which is more than a luxury today. That is the reason why the concentrations of pollutants should be very small in air when compared to the corresponding concentrations in water. A concentration of more than 0.3 mg/1 or 3,00,000 mg/m^3, of lead in water is considered harmful to man but a concentration of 1.5 mg/m^3 of lead in air is deadly harmful.

Effects of Air Pollution on Environment

The centre for Science and Environment updated the estimate and found that the situation had worsened as a person was dying for every 53 minutes because of air pollution, especially due to diesel run vehicles in India.

Majority of air pollutants like sulphur dioxide, nitrogen dioxide, ozone, ammonia etc. have a direct effect on man, material and vegetation. Air pollution can affect the environment on a global scale. Carbon dioxide as a green house gas causes global warming, increases mean sea level, submerges millions of hectares of fertile land and brings famine thus leading eventually to destruction of life on this planet. Sulphur dioxide and nitrogen dioxide can bring acid rains which can completely upset the delicate balance between the various biotic and abiotic components of the biosphere. The Chlorofluorocarbons (CFCs) can destroy the ozone layer; man's protecting umbrella, and spread incurable diseases among human beings and other animals. PAN and other oxidants can completely destroy vegetation. These pollutants one way or other, have already damaged the art treasures and cultural and heritage of man. The Parthenon of Athens to our Taj Mahal, all art treasures withstood the ravages and plunders of the fury of nature for centuries but are showing signs of decay due to atmospheric pollution in this century. It is no hyperbole to say that if man continues his activities of discharging thousands of tons of a variety pollutants into the atmosphere he would be left with no breathing spaces for tomorrow and needs a sanctuary to protect him! A proper place for a sanctuary also may be beyond his reach.

The success or failure of respiratory defense system depends, in part upon the size of the particulates inhaled and the depth of their penetration into the respiratory tract. About 40 per cent of the particles 1-2 um in size are retained in bronchioles and alveoli particles ranging in size from 0.25 to 1 um show a decrease in retention. Little information is available on the detrimental effects of particulate matter on vegetation. Dry cement kiln dust appears to cause little damage if deposited on a leaf surface, yet in the presence of moisture, such dust imparts damage and consequential growth inhibition to plant tissues. The dust coating on leaves reduces photosynthesis and the increased plugging of stomata reduces plant growth. Particulate matter can damage materials by soiling clothing and textiles, corroding metals, eroding building surfaces, and discoloring and destroying paint surfaces.

"No need to commit suicide if there is carbon monoxide". 'CO' is very dangerous for human health. This slow poison is odorless, colorless and nonirritating. The affinity of CO is 200 times greater than that of oxygen and hence the body tissues are deprived of their oxygen supply. SO_2 irritates mucous membrane and damages the respiratory tract. Hydrocarbons are known to be carcinogenic. The most significant particulates are bacteria, lead, mercury and asbestos. SO_4 particulates are responsible for reducing visibility by 80 Per cent in U.S.A. In Mexico City, for more than 50 per cent of the particulates, the origin is 'human faces'. Lead of petrol generated from automobiles is a neurotoxin and a metabolic poison. Its accumulation causes mental retardation in 20 per cent of the children who often like lead fumes. 'Mercury' is released into the atmosphere by the fungicides in the paints, coal based power plants and incinerators burning batteries from houses etc. Mercury fumes (<2um) damage respiratory tissues. Asbestos dusts and cigarette smoke are carcinogenic. Cigarette smoke increases 10 times the desire for sex but also decreases the efficiency of participation in sex by 100 times. Photochemical smog has the acrid and biting odor of ozone, brownish colour of NO_2, toxicity of CO and turbidity of smoke. In urban areas, astronomers cannot observe sky and its stars due to light pollution from buildings, dust pollution, outdoor advertisements etc.

Materials are damaged by air pollution by abrasion, chemical action, absorption, adsorption, corrosion or by deposition and removal. Factors such as temperature, precipitation, sunlight, humidity, air movement, stability of atmosphere and mainly the concentration and duration of pollutant play a vital role in the damaging action. Textiles loss their tensile strength due to SO_2 and are soiled by SPM i.e. Suspended Particulate Matter. H_2S and SPM damage paints; SO_2 causes discoloration and embrittlement of paper and leather; wood is softened by ammonia; metals are corroded by acidic mists, chromium and SO_2; oxidants like O_3, PAN, NH_3, and NO_2 cause cracking of rubber while SO_X, NO_X and H_2S can affect even the miniature electronic circuits, solid state devices and computers and high voltage wires and electrical insulations.

Air Pollution in India

The National Environmental Engineering Research Institute (NEERI) has established air monitoring stations in Mumbai, Kolkatta, Chennai, Hyderabad, Kanpur, Jaipur, Ahmedabad and Nagpur in order to measure control of air pollution in India.

The surveys reported that air pollution by sulphur dioxide is highest is Bombay and air pollution by suspended particulate matter is highest in Delhi.

Another study of NEERI reveals a gradual but steady increase in levels of Suspended Particulate Matter (SPM) in Kolkatta since 1977 with 9.6 per cent increase since 1970.

The Global Environmental Monitoring System (GEMS) also reports highest SPM concentration in Kolkatta during 1976-1980. On Dec 2nd -3rd, 1984 Bhopal witnessed an unprecedented tragedy caused by massive leakage of methye-iso-cyanate (MIC) from the

Union Carbide pesticide plant MIC was used by the plant to produce saving, a pesticide.

To control air pollution, in India, the 42nd Amendment of the constitution has provided under articles 48A and 51A the legal foundation of environmental protection. Further the air (prevention and control or pollution) Act 1981, prescribes emission standards for air polluting industries.

In the Panchayat Raj system, health is the responsibility of the Zilla Parishad (ZP). The Primary Health Centres (PHCs) with its sub centres should serve as a focal point through which integrated curative preventive and promotive health care should be provided to the entire population, especially to the families below the poverty line, under its jurisdiction (N.S. Deodhar, 2000). As in the case of the sub-centres, primary health centres may require jurisdictional adjustments to facilitate better service quality and coverage. It is important to recognize that, at present, most of the primary health centres do not function properly.

Conclusion

The Central Pollution Control Board (CPCB) is the national apex body for assessment, monitoring and control of water and air pollution. The executive responsibilities for enforcement of the Acts for Prevention and Control of Pollution of Water (1974) and Air (1981) and also of the Water (Cess) Act, 1977 are carried out through the Board. Twenty-three states and union territories have already adopted the Act and respective state pollution control boards have been constituted.

Enactment of the Environment (Protection) Act, 1986, has further extended the scope of the activities of the Board. Under the E (P) Act, 1986, effluent and emission standards in respects of 55 specific industries have been notified. So far, 84 laboratories have been recognized as environmental laboratories. Minimum National Standards (MINAS) for effluents and emissions from specific industries have been formulated and control measures are being implemented in a phased manner.

Seventeen categories of heavily polluting industries have been identified namely, cement, thermal power plants, distilleries, sugar, fertilizer, integrated iron and steel, oil refineries, pulp and paper, petro-chemicals, pesticides, tanneries, basic drugs and pharmaceuticals, dye and dye intermediates, caustic soda, zinc smelter, copper smelter and aluminium smelter. Action is taken against the defaulting units in these categories on priority. On the basis of the designated best use of criteria CPCB has identified 13 grossly polluted stretches of Sabarmati, Subernarekha, Godavari, Krishna, Indus (tributaries), Sutlej, Ganga (tributaries), Yemuna, Hindon, Chambal, Damodar, Gomato and Kali rivers to formulate short-term result-oriented programmes. The Ministry, in consultation with state governments, has identified 19 critically polluted areas in the country which need special attention for control of pollution. These are Vapi (Gujarat), Singrauli (UP), Korba (Madhya Pradesh), Digboi (Assam), Talcher (Orissa), Bhadravati (Karnataka), Howrah (West Bengal), Dhanbad (Bihar), Pali (Rajasthan); Manali (Tamil Nadu); Visakhapatnam (Andhra Pradesh), Chembur (Maharashtra), Najafgarh (Delhi); Govindhgarh (Punjab) and Udyog Mandal (Kerala). The progress in abatement of pollution in these areas is being reviewed from time to time.

References

B.N. Ahuja, "Advanced Essays for College and Competitive Exams", Goodwill Publishing House, New Delhi.

C.S. Rao, "Environmental Pollution Control Engineering", Whiley Eastern Ltd, New Delhi, 1991.

Cunningham P., Willium and Barbara W. Saigo, "Environmental Science", 3rd Edition, Wm.C.Brown Publishers, Dubuque, USA, 1995.

IUCNN Publications of 2002 (International Union for Conservation of Nature and Natural Resources).

K.V.S.G. Murali Krishna, "Air Pollution and Control", Kaushal & Company, Kakinada, 1999.

K.V.S.G. Murali Krishna, "Atmospheric Pollution", Monthly Telugu Academy, Hyderabad, July 1993.

Khopkar, S.M., "Environmental Pollution analysis", New Delhi: New Age International Ltd, 1995.

Kiran B., Chhokar, Mamata Pandya, Meena Raghunathan, 'Understanding Economics', sage Publications India private Limited.

KVSG Murali Krishna, 'Glimpses of Environment', Environmental Protection Society, Kakinada.

Laura Carlsen, Indigenous Communities in Latin America: Fighting for Control of Natural Resources in a Globalised Age, Americas Program, (Silver City, NM: Interhemispheric Resource Center).

Mehta, S.S. Munale and U. Sankar, "Controlling Pollution: Incentives and regulations, Sage Publications, New Delhi, 1997.

16

Global and National Environmental Protection Policies

Introduction

Environment is simply defined as all those conditions and influences surrounding a living being and affecting its existence and development. And environmental economics is concerned with the impact of economy on the environment, the significance of environment to the economy and appropriate way of regulating economic activity so that balance is achieved among environment, economic and other social goals.

The essence of environmental problem is economy-producer behaviour and consumer desires; without economy most environmental issues are simply questions of concern to chemist or biologist with no policy significance.

Environment and Development

There is a close relationship between environment and development. All the basic resources required for human living and development come from the environment. It is the environment that provides raw materials to the industries, food for our people, fodder for our cattle, fuel for our transport etc., and the environment also absorbs the waste that our developmental activity creates.

That is the environment acts both as a resource and as a sink for our developmental activity. For example Inland Water bodies are a source of fish, water for irrigation etc., for village economies. They also act as a sink for excess fertilizer and pesticides that may runoff from the agriculture fields. This is the reason why we cannot look at development is isolation from environment which it supports. This calls for our immediate attention to initiate effective measures to protect our environment which promotes sustained living of the human beings on this planet. An attempt is made here to present measures, in brief, initiated both at the global and the national level towards environmental protection.

Measures to Protect Environment

1. All industries should follows safe and scientific methods of disposing the waste materials;
2. Industries polluting the atmosphere should be closed down;
3. Instead of chemical fertilizers, the use of manures on large-scale has to be encouraged; and Afforestation and planting of saplings in urban and rural areas are to be taken upon large-scale so as to restore the levels of oxygen in our atmosphere and also prevent several natural hazards.

Global Initiatives for Environmental Protection

It is universally acknowledged that people all over the world are highly concerned of the fast deteriorating environmental and ecological balances resulting in serious health hazards to the extent of threatening the safe sustained existence of mankind. Hence, governments of the nations of the world have initiated steps towards environmental protection. Some of the most important initiatives in this regard are listed as below:

1. The first world conference on the environment was held in Stockholm, Sweden, in 1972 under the auspices of the United Nations.
2. UNEP Nairobi declaration 1982.
3. Vienna convention (Ozone Layer Problems), 1985.
4. Montreal Protocol 1987.
5. Publication of Price Report-Blue prints for a green economy, 1989 (in which the notable polluter pays principle was propounded).
6. In 1982, the third environment conference sponsored by the United Nations was held in Rio de Janeiro, Brazil. Popularly called the Earth Summit, and formally the conference environment and Development.

7. Rio conference 1992 where a detailed action plans has been drawn up maintaining hazard free environment.
8. In December 1997, delegates from nearly 160 nations participated in a U.N. Summit on global warming held in Kyoto, Japan. During the conference, delegates approved a legally binding treaty for countries to reduce emission of green house gases.
9. In the year 2000, IPCC issued its third assessment record stating that "most of the observed warming over the last fifty years is likely to have been due to the increase in green house gas concentration".
10. World Summit on Sustainable Development was held on May 15, 2002 in pairs, releases the UNEP's over view report 10 years after Rio.

Environmental Protection Initiatives in India

The Independent India is well aware of the fact that the poverty is the biggest threat to conservation of natural resources. The population of India which was little over 35 crore at the time of Independence has reached an all time high figure of 110 crore by July, 2005 that means the population of India increased by more than three folds over a period of 58 years. It is well-nigh impossible to feed the ever increasing population without indulging in environmental degradation in terms of over using the natural resources such as converting the rain forest area into form lands. Not with standing these constraints the Government of India initiated measures to protect environment. Some of the most important initiatives in this regard are listed as below:

1. Wild Life Protection Act, 1972.
2. The Water Prevention and Control of Pollution Act 1974, amended in 1988.
3. The Air (Prevention and Control of Pollution) Act 1981, amended in 1987.
4. The Water (Prevention and Control of Pollution) Cess Act 1981, amended in 1987.
5. Forest conservation Act, 1986.

6. The Environment (Protection) Act, 1986.
7. Motor Vehicle Act, 1936, amended in 1988.
8. Public Liability Insurance Act, 1991.
9. The Factories Act, 1947.
10. Hazardous Waste (Management and Handling Rules) 1989.
11. The establishment of National Council of Environment Planning and Co-operation in 1972, under developmental Science and Technology. In 1980 separate department of Environment was set up.
12. In Year 1985 Ministry of Environment and Forests was setup to interact with Government on planning, promotion and co-ordination of Environment and forestry programs.
13. The Ministry of Surface Transport has notified rules relating to registration of non-commercial vehicle and introduced Euro Norms. Mashelkar Committee on National Auto Fuel Policy recommended introducing Euro-III by 2005 and Euro-IV by 2010.
14. Central Pollution Control Board has been setup. It is the National Apex body for assessment, monitoring and control of pollution. It advises the central government. On all matters concerning the prevention and control of air, water and noise pollution and also provides technical services to ministry for implementing the provisions of Environment Protection act, 1986.
15. Environmental Impact Assessment Programme has been setup for the purpose of evaluation of project or a programme, which is likely to cause damage to environment.
16. Environment Education and Information Programme was launched. In this programme priority has been accorded by the environment ministry to promote environmental education among the various age groups and to disseminate information through environment information system (ENVIS) network to all concerned.
17. An Eco-mark label has been introduced to label consumer products that are environment friendly and eco-mark criteria for 16 product categories covering approximately 450

products have been finalized and notified.

18. Eco-development programme was introduced which aims at the restoration of already degraded ecosystem through practical scheme, such as land reclamation, afforestation, cleaning of water bodies etc.,

Conclusion

The Government of India has released draft relating to National Environmental Policy of 2004. With a view to ensuring planning, promotion, co-ordination and overseeing the implementation of various schemes relating to environment and forest. The central objective of the policy is conservation of critical environmental resources. The draft maintains that conserving ecological system is essential for life support, livelihoods, economic growth and a broad conception of human being.

This apart the apex court-Supreme Court expressed its concern with regard to environmental degradation. It directly advised the government that it should anticipate, prevent and remedy the cause of environmental degradation and that the financial burden for the environmental protection should not be shifted to taxpayer but the polluter should pay. This clearly reflects the judicial commitment to recognize the right to humane and healthy environment as an essential facet of Article 21 of the constitution of India.

Form the foregone discussion that environment supports the life of each individual on the planet. It is, therefore, the bonded duty of each individual to protect environment that sustains us. If we wish to live a healthy life, undoubtly, we need a healthy environment. The achievement of this goal will demand the acceptance of responsibility by citizens, communities, enterprises and at every level, and sharing equitably in common efforts. As people who are concerned of environmental protection should necessarily reorient their lives patterns by minimizing the use of fissile fuel, electricity, pesticides, fertilizers, coal, polythin bags, plastic containers, explosives and highly combustible elements and encourage exploring and exploiting more of non-conventional sources of energy, viz, solar, wind and sea-waves. The reoriented life pattern is assumed to take one closer to nature; on the other hand starts preserving and conserving environment.

The article concludes by stating that it's not the governments alone that should take care of environmental protection but it should be taken as the responsibility of every one that live on the planet. The governments, apart from doing their own share of work in this regard, should educate the people through intensive awareness camps about environmental problems which if unattended would prove to be more dangerous than social and economic problems in the near future.

References

C.S.O. 2000, "Compendium of Environmental Statistics 2000", pp 287-291.

Charles. D Kolstad "Environmental Economics".

Chhatwal, G.R. Encyclopedia of Environmental Water Pollution, Anmol Publications Pvt. Ltd., pp. 816-818.

Dave, L.G. "Social Accounting", Renuka Publishers, pp 101-110, 2001.

Khoshoo, T.N. "Environmental concerns and strategies", Ashish Publication House, New Delhi.

Kumar, Satish, "Protecting Environment: A Quest for NGOs, Kalinga Publications, 1999.

Kumar, Shivendra "Environmental Control" Chanyaka Civil Services Today", Vol.5, No.1, 2004, pp 152-154.

Patil, R.B. and Pawar, S.N. Sociology of Environment, Rawat Publications pp 227-228, 1995.

Sudharshan, K. Cherry and Trivedi, P.R. "Global Environmental Issues", Commonwealth Publishers, pp 230-235, 1995.

The Hindu "Survey on Environment 2003".

17

Effects of Water Pollution on Human Health

Introduction

Water is a basic need of life. Yet, about 80 per cent of people inhabiting the rural regions of the developing world in general and India in particular have no access the safe drinking water. The non-availability of safe drinking water has a direct bearing on the level of health of the people and their capacity for doing work. Importance of drinking water to human beings can be realized from the fact that two –thirds of the human body consists of water. A reduction of 10 per cent in this water comment of the body can causes serious disorders and a reduction of 20 per cent can cause death. An attempt is made here to analyse the health hazards due to consumption of fluoride water in Anantapur district in addition to explain causes and consequences of water pollution.

Water Resources

Water is important to the survival of human, plant and animal life. Earth is the only planet in the planetary system endowed with water resources. Nearly 80 per cent of the earth's system is covered with water in the form of oceans, lakes, and rivers etc. The oceans contain most of the water, nearly 97 per cent of the total water and cover most of the water surface on earth. The rest is fresh water and at any time, about 22 per cent of fresh water is stored under the surface of the earth as ground water and the rest is stored in ice caps and glaciers. The water is precious and needs in almost all human activities, irrigation, industry, mining, power generation and domestic and so on.

Sector-wise utilization of total water resources in India (1997) reveals the fact that nearly 83 per cent of the available water is being consumed by agriculture sector for providing irrigational facilities to increase the productivity levels in both food crops and non-food crops in the country; around 5 per cent of water is being utilised for domestic purposes while an equal percentage of 3.3 is being independently shared by industries and power generation plants.

Much of the water is stored in oceans and this water undergoes evaporation by solar energy. High winds distribute water vapour around the globe. Water gets condensed on to the land in the form of rain, snow and fog and supports land based eco-systems. All living organisms need water for their survival and water is responsible for metabolic processes within cells so as to maintain nutrient flow in eco-systems.

Water Pollution

Definition: The presence of unwanted and harmful substances in water is called water pollution. Water is a universal solvent i.e. it dissolves many substances in it. This property is mainly responsible for the pollution of water. Water pollution was noticed first by Hippocrates.

The main water pollutants are: Petroleum, DDT, Insecticides, Pesticides, heavy metals like mercury, Cadmium, Arsenic, Fertilizers, Nuclear wastes, human wastes, Dyes, Soaps, Detergents, Sediments, Sewage, Fluoride and heat etc.

Water is the very vital resource for the survival of life and the extent of this resource has already been explained. Such an important component of earth's system is being polluted.

There is an adequate fresh water to maintain one more population doubling on global basis, given the present usable patterns. India is rich in rainfall and surface water resources. India has a very low capital availability of drinking water. According to one realistic estimate more than 40,000 villages in the country may not be having drinking water.

Pollution of water is alerting of its quality so that it becomes unfit or less fit for the purpose for which its natural state is used. Water pollution occurs when chemicals or nutrients or wastes enter water faster than they can be removed by natural process.

Causes and Consequences of Water Pollution

Causes of Water Pollution

1. Firstly, community wastes for human settlements give rise to water pollution. Contrary to the common brief, it has been estimated that the community wastes "account for four times as much waste water as industrial effluents".
2. Secondly, industrial effluents directly entering into a stream or through a municipal sewer or through a discharge on land meant for irrigation causes water pollution.
3. Thirdly, anything stored on earth, such as, any raw materials, solid refuse of a mine or quarry on any land may cause pollution by rain washing it into a stream.
4. Fourthly, the use of fertilizers also causes water pollùtion when unused nitrogenous fertilizers are drained out of soil into lakes and rivers.
5. Fifthly, water pollution may also be caused by air pollutant.
6. Sixthly, Fluoride in groundwater.

Consequences of Water Pollution

More than a billion people in developing countries lack access to clean water; more than 2 billion have no access to basic sanitation. Five to Six million people, mostly children, die every year to water pollution and air pollution.

It is estimated that many countries will have fresh water storage by 2025. Owing to water pollution two-thirds of world population may live in water stressed conditions. Depletion to groundwater has been causing alarming situation. There is no judicious use of water in many countries and much of the water is wasted. Dams may ensure a year round water supply, but much water gets evaporated and experiences loss due to seepage.

The immediate effect scarcity of safe water for drinking purposes. Nearly one billion people worldwide lack access to safe drinking water. In many large cities in the developing countries, the drinking water supply is polluted. In South East Asia, only 550 million people have access to safe drinking water!

Water-borne diseases, also known as dirty-water diseases result from consuming contaminated water. Around 2.3 billion people globally suffer from these diseases. The polluted water contains water-borne pathogens or protozoa. An Estimated 12 million deaths occur every year, five million of them due to diarrhea diseases. Most of these victims are children from developing countries. Around 60-70 working days are lost in a year on a average due to water borne diseases resulting in leave applications.

Water pollution affects the food production also. Agriculture it self pollutes water due to the usage of fertilizers, pesticides and herbicides. The effect of water pollution on fisheries is very severe because the depletion of oxygen in the water due to the presence of toxic and organic wastes kills fish.

The chemical, plastic and paper industries release wastes containing mercury into rivers which merge into oceans. Since the mercury levels in these wastes are more than normal, some types of fish in the coastal waters contain more mercury in their bodies, when people consume this fish, they become seriously ill or die.

Even industries have problem with polluted water. They generally use soft water for most of the applications and treating contaminated water to make it fit for use becomes costly.

The waste heats in the enables it useless for industrial cooling purposes.

A Public Health Disaster in Andhra Pradesh

According to the Government of Andhra Pradesh own statistics, villagers in over 33,000 rural settlements do not have access to safe drinking water.

Of these, over 3,000 settlements do not even have one source of safe drinking water, as almost all have high levels of fluoride. Data with the Rajiv Gandhi National Drinking Water Mission (RGNDWM) shows that Andhra Pradesh has 7,548 habitations with excess fluoride in drinking water while the general groundwater broad estimates the number of people consuming water with fluoride in excess of 1.5 ppm/litre at 12,70,000.

another 16,00,000 consume water with fluoride content above one ppm/litre but below 1.5 ppm/litre. In some villages of Nalgonda, fluoride content of over seven and eight ppm/litre has been recorded, while the maximum recorded in drinking water has been 83.5 ppm/litre.

But Nalgonda is merely the most visible face of the devastation caused by excess fluoride in drinking water. But in the opinion of D. Nuralidharan of the National Geophysical Research Institute (NGRI), Andhra Pradesh is not the worst affected by fluoride when compared to Rajasthan, with a frightening 16,560 villages has half of India's fluoride-affected villages. Gujarat has 2,378 villages, Orissa 1,138 villages, Uttar Pradesh 1,072 villages and Karnataka 860 out of 17 states that have fluoride affected habitations. The government of India classifies 15 States are having an endemic fluoride problem.

India, in any case, is only one of the 28 countries identified by UNICEF as having a serious public health problem associated with fluoride in drinking water. Dr. Muralidharan says that this is a common problem in the "semi-arid tropics", where drinking water is mostly sourced from under the ground during the long spells. But fluoride in drinking water is also becoming a continuous public health issue in temperate countries like the US and Canada, where water is sourced primarily from rivers and lakes and fluoride is added to water as a deliberate policy of dental health. According to UNICEF, India has produced some of the most comprehensive research and data regarding the dangers of fluoride in drinking water. A point also stressed by Dr. Muralidharan of NGRI and Nalgonda was the focus of an ambitious project to provide fluoride-free water through the "flocculation" method.

Anantapur district, in the Rayalaseema region has many more fluoride affected villages as do Nalgonda, Karimnagar, Prakasam, Guntur, Mahaboobnagar and Kadapa also have a fair number.

With the groundwater getting deeper and deeper into the soils, the percentage of fluoride content in the water has shot-up rapidly in Anantapur district. More than 210 villages in Kadiri and

Nallamada constituents are caught in the grip of high percentage of fluoride. The consumption of fluoride water has resulted in many health hazards, such as, deformed bones and bent backbones, deformed skulls and stunted physical growth of human beings.

People have been highly scared to fluoride water in the district. As matter of fact the sacred people have left few habitations, such as, chandrayudupalli in Mudigubba mandal and Kodavalavandlapalli in Numbalapulakuntla mandal.

The fluoride content in water has been ranging from 2.92 to 4.8 ppm/litre in the above referred places. But it is learned that there is no harm if one consumes water, which has fluoride content, ranging between 1.5 to 2 ppm/litre. The consumption water which consists of fluoride above 2 ppm/litre will result in severe health hazards and unbearable body pains for all the age-groups rendering them unfit for any worthwhile works.

It is rather surprising to notice that fluoride content reported to be 9 ppm/litre in Nandivaripalli and Settivaripalli in Obuladevulacheruvu mandal in addition to another 9 villages where the fluoride content in water is above 8 ppm/litre which calls for a considerable concern to provide safe drinking water to save the lives of these people from fluorosis, a diseases that has affected one and all irrespective of age differentials.

As in the case of other districts where fluoride playing havoc with lives of the people, here also in Anantapur district, the State Government and Local bodies has not done anything worthwhile to safe guard the people from fluorosis. It is high time that the Government and Local bodies and NGO's to come forward with comprehensive plans to launch schemes to provide fluoride-free water in the rural areas of the 7 districts of Andhra Pradesh - Anantapur, Nalgonda, Karimnagar, Prakasam, Guntur, Mahaboobnagar and Kadapa. For 80 per cent of the diseases in these rural areas are attributed to unsafe drinking water. Therefore, all those concerned may give a serious thought to provide safe drinking water in all the fluoride affected villages in the 7 districts of A.P. by spending a considerable amount. For expenditure incurred one the provisions of safe drinking water in the areas tantamount to expenditure incurred, indirectly, on health maintenance.

References

C. Manoharacharya and P. Jayarami Reddy, "Principles of Environmental Studies", B.S. Publications, 4-4-309, Girirajhane, Sultan Bazar, Hyderabad.

Eenadu, Anantapur Edition, Anantapur District Special dated: 06-01-2005, Anantapur.

N. Manivaskam, "Environmental Pollution", National Book Trust India, New Delhi, 1984.

R.K. Sapru, "Environment Management in India", (Vol.1), Ashish Publishing House, New Delhi.

Rajeev Grag, "Environmental Quiz Book", Pustak Mahal, Delhi.

S.A. Sali, "Resources for Future Economic Growth", Vikas Publishing House Pvt. Ltd., New Delhi.

S.K. Shukla and P.R. Srivastava, "Environmental Resources Conservation", Commonwealth Publishers, New Delhi.

Sumanjeet,, "Environmental Degradation & Protection", Vision, Vol. XXI No.1-2, July-December 2004, Journal of the Jayaprakash Narayan, Institute of Social & Economics Studies Bubaneswar, India.

The Hindu, "Survey of the Environment", 2004, the Hindu.

18

Strategies for Sustainable Development

"We still have to learn how to live peacefully not only with our fellow men, but also with nature" -- Schumacher

"As the custodians of nature, we all have a duty to use the power of science, engineering and technology, with humility and reverence, to preserve and protect our 'rare earth'. As 'ecofeminists', we need to develop a positive attitude towards nature-let us see life as cooperation rather than competition, a network of personal relationships rather than isolated egos and environment as bounty rather than scarcity. Let us all develop a strong sense of love, respect and reverence for mother nature. Let us all unite in the cause of our 'one earth' with 'Environment' as our common religion-controlling influence on one's life-Let nature rule our hearts". (Source: Glimses of Environment - Dr. KVSG Murali Krishna, p.247).

Introduction

Sustainable Development: Development is a process that cannot be stopped and should not be stopped. The qualitative and quantitative developments of human activity, with the advent of science and technology have hitherto been giving positive benefits. Of late resource depletion and ecological degradation are mounting up as unwanted by-products of man's development, thereby projecting gloomy prospects for the future of man. In this context sustainable development has become the loud slogan of the day. Sustainable development implies the following factors. -

1. Natural resources should be continuously available for man's activities for an indefinite period.
2. Man's scientific and technological achievements should continue to improve the comfort and quality of life.
3. Social disparities and inequalities of opportunities should not

increase, as seems to be happening in the present day development. For example, if a few people can afford open

4. Heart surgery while allowing millions of deaths every year due to water borne diseases, the type of development is not sustainable.
5. Sustainable development should ensure the preservation of ecological diversity and stability. Man's health and happiness should not be reduced by the developmental processes.
6. The damage already suffered by the present level of development should be undone to the best possible extent.

Concept of Sustainable Development

The concept of sustainable development is of origin and has been a serious concern across the globe. The first conference on human environment was held in 1972 at Stockholm. Changes in atmosphere chemistry, air pollution, acid rain, ozone depletion and the buildup of green house gases have attracted the attention of scientists and the general public. Earth temperature has begun an upward climb.

An environmental consequence of climatic change is giving way to deepening concern. People are starting to realize that if this irreplaceable resource is lost, much of the earth's diversity of plant and animal life would also disappear. In this context economic development policies that are not environmentally sustainable are doomed to failure. Indeed the concept sustainable development has gained wide spread acceptance.

It is pertinent to recall here the report of the world commission on Environment and development released in April 1997 says that "Earth is one but world is not" we all depend on one biosphere for sustaining our lives. Yet each community, each country strives for survival and prosperity with little regard for its impact on other? The UN conference on environment and development was held in Brazil in 1992 where 166 world countries participated. As public awareness of population arithmetic energy policies and environmental trends threatening to undermine the human prospect has become more wide spread.

The public awareness is needed.

Environment and development are not the too separate entities but linked together in a complex system of cause and effect. Environmental problems arise both lacks of development and from unprotected and unintended consequences of economic growth. It is a byproduct of modem development, growth and equity. Advanced countries because of over consumption leading to enormous amounts of garbage acid rain pollution etc. The World Commission Environment and Development warned about the problem of industrial waste management challenging us as a society and wanted as much care to be taken for present and succeeding generations as for those in the distinct future. Governments have failed to cope-up with these challenges. Thus environmental concerns have assumed significance in the recent years. Commensurate with industrial expansion a strong regulatory mechanism is required to ensure minimum environmental standards.

As per the traditional theory Economic Development refers to a process of economic transformation involving the structural transformation of an economy through industrialization and improvement in the quality of human lives; it has three aspects:

1. raising people's living levels;
2. improvement in institutional framework of the economy; and
3. increasing people's freedom to choose by enlarging varieties of consumer goods and services.

The recent concept of development refers to sustainable development which not only aims at development but also to protect the environment. Sustainability refers to both ecological and economic attributes. Sustainable development as defined by the World Commission on Environment and Development (WCED) requires boundary condition to be satisfied do as to take care of the considerations of intergenerational equity in resource use. The word sustainable development is the total development of the society, economic changes, social and cultural transformation taking into consideration the social well being and security of all the sections. Sustainability is the conservation which requires that stock of individual resources should not be declining over time. Sustainable development the concept of enhancing the living conditions while ensuring the stream of future consumption rates to be atleast the same as of now can be taken as the most acceptable guiding principle. Sustainability means preservation of the productivity and full functioning of natural resource base.

Approaches to Sustainable Development

To meet the rising needs of the rising population within the limitations imposed by sustainable development, the efforts needed are immense and multidimensional. The primary needs of sustainable development are:

- Environmental awareness
- Modified eco-friendly technology
- Determination and will at the individual national and international level and
- Cooperation and coordination.

As technology develops, issues tend to be more globalised. The future of the concept of sustained development depends largely on a global coordination. Fortunately, the international conventions on environmental issues held in Stockholm, Geneva, Rio etc., indicate the global movement in the right direction, before it is too late. As it is, the present global damage is reversible and further damage is preventable, provided the appropriate measures are taken up seriously.

Measures for Sustainable Development

1. **Population control:** Sustainable human population in each area should be estimated and growth should be limited to the desirable level.
2. **Reduced consumption:** Values of life should be shifted to honor lesser consumption and simpler life styles. Mental development should gain more respect than material pomp.
3. **Integrated Land use Planning:** Relative priorities among different land uses like agriculture, forestry, fodder

cultivation, urban and industrial growths, traffic etc., should be planned and managed judiciously.

4. **Water Resource Management:** River flooding and meandering, silting up of natural and man made reservoirs, over exploitation of ground water, water logging by over irrigation and poor drainage and pollution of the water bodies are some of the consequences of poor water resource management. Sustained development implies optimum management of water resources locally and globally.
5. **Renewable Resources:** Future development should be based on material resources that can be renewed or recycled, or resources that cannot be depleted in the near future. For example, wood scan be consumed and can be gown maintaining a balance between the two. Metals can be used, recycling the scrap again and again. Solar energy will not be depleted in the near future and is an ideal energy source.
6. **Biosphere Conservation:** Man's activities or callousness result in the destruction of species. Thousands of plant and animal species are endangered today with threats of extinction due to pollution, destruction of habitat, commercial exploitation, pampering mono cultures etc. To ensure ecological stability, species diversity is essential. Sustained development includes biosphere conservation.
7. **Production Efficiency:** The current production processes involve wastages that can be reduced or avoided or avoided. Better planning and improved technology can lead to better yields from given resources. Genetic hybrids, drip irrigation, pest control, soil-crop-fertility management etc., are examples of improving agricultural productivity.
8. **Pollution Control:** Pollution of air, water and soil constitutes a major threat for future mankind. Improved pollution control technology is another major component of sustainable development.

Thus, the main measures for sustainable development are:

- Removing subsidies that encourage excessive use of fossil furls, pesticides, minerals, timber, water etc,

- Encourage, Educate, Empower and involve local people, rural youth and women in their own long-term interests.
- Protect natural habitats and their biodiversity by protecting estuaries, mangroves, wetlands, forest, mountains etc.

Thus, it is the compatibility between ecology and economics; reaction and anticipation; industry and environment; conservation and exploitation; disposing and recycling; penalties and incentives and curing and prevention. Gro Harlem Brundtland, the first woman Prime Minister of Norway is the pioneer of the concept of "sustainable development".

The purpose of this article is to spell out in brief strategies for sustainable development.

Strategies for Sustainable Development

Use of Non-conventional Sources of Energy: General trend so far has been to produce electricity in thermal and hydro power plants. Both of these have adverse environmental impacts. Thermal power plants emit large quantities of carbon dioxide which is a green house gas. It also produces fly ash which if not used properly can cause pollution of water bodies, land and other components of environment. Also, coal mining affects the environment in various ways. Hydroelectric projects inundate forest and interface with the natural flow of water in the catchments areas and the river basins. As already mentioned, large size projects may also lead to displacement of population from the affected areas. Wind power and solar rays are good examples of non conventional but cleaner and greener technologies.

LPG, Gobar Gas in Rural Areas: Households in rural areas generally use wood, dung cake or other biomass as fuel. This practice has several adverse implications. It leads to deforestation, reduction in green cover, wastage of cattle dung and air pollution. To rectify the situation subsidized LPG is being provided. In addition, gobargas plants are being provided through easy loan and subsidy. As far as liquefied petroleum gas (LPG) is concerned it is a clean fuel. As a result household pollution is reduced to a large extent. Also, energy wastage is minimized. With gobargas plant the cattle dung is fed to the gas plant. Gas is produced which is used as fuel while the slurry which is left over is a very good organic fertilizer and soil conditioner.

CNG in Urban Areas: In Delhi, the use of compressed natural gas (CNG) as fuel in public transport system has significantly lowered air pollution and the air has become cleaner in the last few years.

Wind Power: In areas where speed of wing is usually high, wind mills can provide electricity without any adverse impact on environment. Wind turbines move due to wind and electricity is generated. No doubt, the initial cost is high. But, the benefits are such that the high cost is taken care of readily.

Solar Power through Photovoltaic Cells: We receive large quantity of solar energy in the form of sunlight. We use it in different ways. For example, we dry our cloths, grains, other agricultural products as well as various items made for daily use. We also use it to warm ourselves in winter. Plants use the solar energy to perform photosynthesis. Now, with the help of photovoltaic cells the solar energy can be converted into electricity. These cells use special kind of materials to capture solar energy and to convert the energy into electricity. This technology is extremely useful for remote areas and for places where supply of power through grid or power lines is either not possible or proves very costly. This technique is totally free from pollution.

Mini Hydel Plants: In the mountaineous regions stream can be found almost every where. A large percentage of such streams are perennial. Minihydel plants use the energy of such streams to move small turbines. The turbines generate electricity which can be used locally. Such power plants are more or less environment friendly as they do not change the land use pattern in areas. They generate enough power to meet local demands. So, there is no need for large scale transmission towers and cables and also there is not much transmission loss.

Traditional Knowledge and Practices: Traditionally, Indian people have been close to their environment. They have been behaving as they are a component of the environment and not a controller of the environment. If we look at our agriculture system, healthcare system, housing, transport etc., we find that everything was environment friendly. Only recently we drifted away from the traditional systems and caused large scale damage to the environment and also our rural energy. Now, we are going back. One apt example is of healthcare. Traditionally, we were dependent on natural products for our healthcare. India is very much privileged that it has about 15,000 species of plants which have medicinal properties. About 8,000 off these are in regular use in various systems of treatment including the folk tradition. Due to sudden expansion of western system of treatment, we were ignoring our traditional systems such as Ayurveda, Unani, Tibetan and folk systems of healthcare. However, during last two three decades we have realized their value and we are going back. At present right from hair oil, shampoo, toothpaste body lotion, faircream to almost every type of cosmetic is more herbal than anything else. Similarly, for chronics health problems we depend more and more on Ayurveda, Unani and folk systems of treatment. Not only these are environment friendly, these can also human friendly as these medicines do not lead to side effects, immunity, addition etc. Since large scale industrial & chemical processing are not required.

Bio-composting: In quest to have more and more agricultural production, during last about five decades or so we almost totally neglected the one of compost. We almost completely switched over to chemical fertilizers. Result is that large tracts of productive land has been adversely affected, water bodies including ground water system has suffered due to chemical contamination and demand for irrigation has been going up year by year.

Now, we are going back to our age old tested method of fertilization i.e. use of compost, Now, farmers in large number all over the country are using compost made from organic wastes of different types. In certain parts of the county cattle heads are maintained only because they produce dung which is an important fertilizer and soil conditioner.

Earth owner can convert organic matter into compost faster than normal composting process. They use of composting method is spreading fast all over the country and it is helping the farmers as well as the environment. Indirectly, the civic authorities are benefited too as they have to dispose reduced quality of waste. Waste converted into compost need not be helped by the civic authorities.

Biopest Control: With the advent of green revolution, the entire country entered into a frenzy to use more and more of chemical pesticides to obtain higher yield. Soon, the adverse impacts started showing themselves. Food products were contaminated, soil was polluted, water bodies and even ground water were polluted with pesticides. Even milk, meat and fishes were found to be contaminated.

To meet the challenge efforts are on to bring in better methods of pest control. One such step is use of pesticides based on plant products. Neem trees are proving quite useful. Several types of pest controlling. Chemicals have been isolated from neem and these are being used. Mixed cropping and growing different crops in consecutive years on the same land have also helped the farmers.

In addition awareness is spreading about various animals, and birds which help in controlling pests. For example, snakes are one of the prime groups of animals which prey upon rats, mice and various other pests. In our country only a few types of snakes are poisonous. Rats are harmless. If people can identify the snakes, they will not kill the harmless ones. Similarly, large varieties of birds prey upon vermin and pests. Owl is an apt example. Another well known example is the peacock. If these are allowed to dwell around the agricultural areas, they can clear large varieties of pests including insects. Lizards are also important in this regard. We need to know their value and save them.

Sustainable Development: For Now and Forever

Are we stealing from the future? In many developed and

developing countries, efforts to generate income as fast as possible have damaged natural systems. But future generations, not just the current generation, need those natural systems and what they will produce. Intensive cultivation, clearing forests, filling wetlands, and over fishing-all propelled partly by population growth-eventually can impair the ability of so-called renewable resources to renew themselves. They cannot continue producing, or they produce less. Beyond a certain point, taking more now leaves less for the future.

Development experts and national leaders increasingly recognize that destroying natural systems to meet current needs or to make a quick profit is short-sighted and potentially disastrous for future generations. The alternative-meeting people's current needs while preserving nature's productive capacity for the future-has been termed sustainable development (37, 301).

Adopting the principle of sustainable development requires a fundamental change in thinking. The data used for decision-making must reflect the true costs of resource depletion and pollution as they affect future generations rather than just the short-term costs and profits of depleting income-producing resources (8, 65, 71, 308, and 320). They must take account of future needs on a par with current needs, not "discounted" in a way that weights decisions in favor of short-term results. Sustainable development is an alternative to the "development at any cost" ethos identified with the "drive modernization" of earlier decades.

The concept of sustainable development rejects the conventional view that economic development is a necessity but environmental protection is a luxury. Instead, it argues that long-term economic development and environmental protection are inextricably linked (320). In fact, continued economic development requires the continued productivity of farmlands and forests, adequate and safe water supplies, efficient energy use, and preservation of natural areas for the production of products and for tourism.

2.76=48 per cent (75,139). Going on to measure I-environmental impact-requires additional information on the environmental impact of specific technologies and how they have changed over time.

A simple hypothetical example illustrates the importance of population to environmental impact: Suppose that per capita resource consumption is reduced by 5 per cent, and improved technologies cause 5 per cent less environmental damage. If world population growth continues at its current 1.7 per cent per year, these reductions in environmental impact would be cancelled out in less than six years (274). In reality, the relationships among population size, per capita consumption, and technology are much more complex than the simple I=PxAxT formula suggests. Each of the three factors-population, affluence, and technology-has many different facets, and all three are closely interrelated (138, 158). Also, all three factors are greatly influenced by government economic and social policy.

While the concept of sustainable development seems simple, putting it into practice promises to be difficult. Both political and technical problems abound: Can sustainability be defined on a global basis? How will sustainability be defined and measured for any specific resource? Will nations make major economic policy changes for the world's benefit rather than their own? Can politicians forego offering their constituents short-term benefits in favor of long-term benefits? How should measures of nation's economic well-being reflect sustainability? All these questions and more need serious attention.

Conclusion

It would be a costly mistake if one thinks that Sustainable Development is the sole duty of the governments. On the other hand, it is a consorted effort by each individual to maintain and to manage eco-friendly environment for it guarantees sustainable livelihoods. Thus, in the present context development necessarily implies Sustainable Development which takes care of unhindered supply of required inputs on a sustainable basis without indulging in robbing the resources meant for our future children. Negligence of Sustainable Development sounds death-knell both to the present and the future generations. As such the aforesaid strategies for Sustainable Development are to be meticulously followed for the National welfare.

References

Barbier, EB, 1987, Concept of Sustainable Economic Development, Environment Conservation, 14(2).

Daly H. (1990), "Towards operational principles of sustainable development", Ecological economics.

DB. Varadharajan, 'Sustainable development in India-An environmental safety approach', paper presented at national seminar on Environmental safety held at Hindu college, Guntur, 5-6 March 2003.

KVSG Murali Krishna, (2004), "Glimpses of Environment", Environmental Protection Society, Post Box No.9, Rajeswari Nagar, Kakinada.

Lester, R. Brown, (1988), State of the world, a world watches Report on Progress towards Sustainable Society.

Pearce D.W. and G. Atkinson (1993), "Capital Theory and Measurement of week sustainability", Ecological Economics.

Planning Commission, Economic survey (2002-2003).

Raymond F Mikasell (1992), Environmental Assessment and Sustainability of the project and programme level, World Bank Conference on Environment and Sustainable Development, Washington DC.

WC Ed. (1987), World Commission on Environment and Development on our common feature, Oxford University Press.

19

Biodiversity and Need for its Preservation

"We still have to learn how to live peacefully not only with our fellow men, but also with nature" -- Schumacher

Introduction

The nature provides 4Fs: Food, Fiber, Fuel and Fodder which satisfy basic human needs. After the Industrial Revolution and Green Revolution, man started exploiting nature to a greater extent. As population increased and also the man's desires, the exploitation of nature was on the rise. The consequences that took place in the Post World War period and the present period of New Economic Reforms have resulted in loss of biodiversity, the damage done to environment and ecology has attracted special attention, and there is an urgent need to stop the loss.

Definition

'Biological diversity' or Biodiversity is that part of nature which includes the differences in genes among the individuals of a species; the variety and richness of all the plant and animal species at different scales in space-locally, in a region, in the country and the world; and the types of ecosystems, both terrestrial and aquatic, within a defined area.

Biological diversity deals with the degree of nature's variety in the biosphere. This variety can be observed at three levels – the genetic variability within a species; the variety of species within a community; and the organization of species in an area into distinctive plant and animal communities.

Biological diversity is an important component of our natural resource stock. This has special significance for India, which is the home for rich and varied life forms. Biodiversity forms the backbone of rural livelihood systems, contributing to food security, health care, energy supply and so on. It also acts as source of various artifacts, which provides income.

Biodiversity or biological diversity is the measure of the variety of the Earth's animal, plant, and microbial species; of genetic differences within species; and of the ecosystems that support the species. The maintenance of biodiversity is important for ecological stability. Research suggests that biodiversity is far greater than previously realized, especially among smaller organisms. It is said that only 1 to 10 per cent of the world's bacterial species have been identified.

The importance of preserving biodiversity worldwide can be gauged from the fact that international convention for the preservation of biodiversity was signed by 100 world leaders in 1992.

India's rich biodiversity is estimated to be over 45,000 plant species, representing about 7 per cent of the world's flora; and its bewildering variety of animal life represents 6.5 per cent of world's fauna. Our country is one of the 12 countries identified as mega-centres of biological diversity. Embracing ten bio-geographic zones and 25 biotic provinces, India incorporates an exceptional range of biodiversity, including all the world's major ecosystems.

Between 7 and 9 million square kilometers of tropical rain forests, covering large tracts of Central America, the Amazon basin and the Guianas, West Africa and Zaire, South East Asia, New Guinea and the islands of Melaesia are estimated to be there on the face of the earth. In Central America two thirds of the forests have already disappeared. In Colombia it has been cleared at the rate of a million hectares a year. The tragic story of the rain forests in Brazil is no different. Tropical rain forests are the greatest, most enduring celebrations of life ever to have evolved on this planet. No other environment has so many species of plant and animal life.

Tropical rain forests are the centres of the world; much of the earth's contemporary flora and fauna originated in the humid tropics. For millions of years, tropical rain forests have been factories of evolutionary diversity from which plants and animals, capable of adapting to more difficult environments, have gone forth to populate the subtropical and temperate regions. It is essential to maintain areas of tropical rain forest large enough for this evolution to continue.

At present the forests which embrace a sizeable portion of biodiversity comprise about 64 million hectares, or about 19 per cent of the land area of the country, according to satellite imaging. Roughly 33 per cent of this forest cover represents primary forest. Indian flora comprises about 15,000 flowering plants and bulk of our rich flora is to be found in the North-East, Western Ghats, the North-Western and Eastern Himalayas, and the cooling systems were based on impeding the flow of thermal load into the building to create conditions of comfort. Where such an option is available, this option would be more efficient than removal of heat flux after it entered the building.

The external building fabric is considered as the "Envelope" of the building. The 'Envelope' is used to remove the extra thermal load on the building, without the air entering into the living spaces.

Envelop cooling system is a technique that uses evaporative cooling principle incorporated into the building envelop. The 'envelope' itself is used as a massive evaporative cooler incorporated into the building fabric to reduce internal temperatures within the building. He energy required for the system to function is obtained from renewable sources.

The concept of use of the 'envelope' to act as the evaporative cooler has the advantage that there is no impact of humidity inside the building. The external walls of the building, in this case, can be visualized as continuous air passages acting as a heat exchanger. The entire cooling, therefore, takes place in the shell itself. The construction of a hollow wall in the 'envelope' acts as an air-gap, thus improving the insulating quality of the wall by slowing the heat flow into the building.

An inexhaustible water source provides the medium for cooling. The water is atomized and impelled into the cavity wall.

Unused water is collected at the bottom and recycled so that there is no unnecessary loss of water in the system.

As the extent and efficiency of evaporative cooling is a direct function of the surface area and the rate of air flow, increased surface area demands a lower rate of air flow for the same degree of cooling. The atomized water particles exponentially increase the surface area for evaporative cooling. Hence, the air flow rate is not very demanding in such a system. Dry air enters the building wall, and is removed, expelling the unwanted thermal load from the envelope in a highly efficient manner.

Dehumidification of incoming air is carried out using a desiccant wheel. As the humid air passes through the desiccant, it absorbs the moisture and dries the air. The wet desiccant is heated to about 50 ^{0} C to dry.

Importance of Biodiversity

Biodiversity may sound like an abstract concept, but in reality it touches almost every aspect of our life. The earth has an enormous variety of plants and animals, both domesticated and wild, as also a wide array of habitats and ecosystems. This diversity meets the food, medicinal, clothing, shelter, spiritual as well as the recreational needs of millions of people around the world. It also ensures that ecological functions such as the supply of clean water, nutrient cycling and soil protection are maintained. In fact, biodiversity loss would mean a threat to the survival of the human race. Here an attempt is made to specify reasons for the increased concern about Biodiversity and its loss.

Survival: Quite simply, without biological diversity we would perish. The global collection of genes, species, habitats and ecosystems is our real wealth, far more important than money. Perhaps the most important value of biodiversity, particularly in a country like India, is that it meets the basic survival needs of a vast number of people. Even today a large number of traditional communities depend, wholly or partially, on the surrounding natural resources for their daily needs of food, shelter, clothing, household goods, medicines, fertilizers, entertainment, etc.

Health and Healing: Up to 80 per cent of the people in developing countries depend for primary health care on traditional medicine, most of which is derived from plants, and some from animal and mineral sources.

It is not just traditional medicines that are derived from biotic resources. Nearly one-fourth of all prescription drugs used in the developed world are based on plants. These include 21 drugs which are today almost indispensable – whether it is aspirin from the plant Filipendula ulmaria, or quinine from the bark of several species of the cinchona tree.

Food Security: Biodiversity is critical for agriculture. About 90 per cent of the world's food comes form 20 plant species. Genetic diversity is important in breeding crops and livestock. Crop breeders need a diversity of crop varieties in order to breed new varieties that resist evolving pests and diseases. Modern agricultural practices have replaced genetic diversity in crops and livestock with uniformity, and this could have dangerous consequences. The loss of diversity in crop species has severe implications for global food security. A single pest invasion or disease could wipe out all standing crop or a particular livestock.

Many crops have been 'rescued' with genetic material from wild relatives or traditional varieties. In the early 1970s, genes from a wild rice variety from India helped to save rice crops from total destruction by the widespread grassy stunt virus in many parts of Asia. Scientists at the International Rice Research Institute in the Philippines searched 6,723 samples for a gene resistant to the virus. They found it in only one single sample of Oryza nivara, collected from eastern UP in 1963. The strain of rice evolved by using that sample is now widely grown all over South and South-East Asia.

Aesthetic Pleasure: Each species and ecosystem adds to the richness and beauty of life on earth. Perhaps no artificial medium can match the sheer joy of watching a sunset over an ocean, the sight of a leaping deer, the sound of a singing bird, or the smell of wet earth after the first rains. A natural ecosystem, once destroyed, is impossible to recreate. The number of people who visit a natural site is an indication of its aesthetic value. For example, every year more than 15,00,000 people visit the Sanjay Gandhi National Park on the outskirts of Mumbai.

Ethical Reasons: Each species is unique and has a right to exist. Humans do not have the right to eliminate any species. Ethics provide the basis for deciding what is good or bad, right or wrong. The World Charter for Nature, adopted by the United Nations in 1982, states that 'Every form of life is unique warranting respect regardless of its worth to man, and to accord other organisms such recognition, man must be guided by a moral code of action'.

Ecological Services: Species evolve to fill particular niches (roles) in an ecosystem or habitat. Many species also depend on each other in intricate ways for survival. Destroying one species can lead to further extinctions or changes. Specific life forms present in a particular habitat help to create conditions for other life forms to live in that environment. For example, a single tree provides not only its products, which may have economic value, but it is also a habitat for innumerable living things. In addition, it also plays a vital role in conserving soil and water and helping to keep the air clean. Mangroves and coral reefs, apart from their normal ecosystem service role in preventing erosion, play a critical role in protecting offshore life during hurricanes and storms. These are services for which it is very difficult to put a precise monetary value. Sometimes it is even difficult to know what services a species provides. Most often the price for ecological services thus remains unpaid.

Take the case of Mumbai. A substantial part of Mumbai city's drinking water comes from the Tansa and Borivili reservoirs. These reservoirs are in turn protected by the surrounding forests which are under the wildlife (protection) Act of 1972. Yet Mumbai's citizens do not pay for the upkeep of these forests and reservoirs.

Religious and Cultural Purposes: In India, many plants and animals have ritual significance and are associated with religious, spiritual and other cultural uses. Among the auspicious flowers offered in temples are hibiscus, offered to the goddess Kali, and Datura flowers offered to Shiva. Various plant and animal species are considered sacred on account of their association with different deities. Some animal species are believed to be the vahanas or vehicles of the deities and are hence venerated. Important among these are the bull of Shiva, the rat of Ganesha the lion of Durga and Owl of Goddess Lakshmi.

In India and several other countries, pockets of forests have traditionally been set aside because they are believed to be the abode of a particular god. Over the ages, local communities have protected these areas which are called sacred groves. As a result of the protection, these areas are preserved as pockets of rich biodiversity.

Erosion of India's Biodiversity

India's rich biological diversity is rapidly eroding. At least 10 per cent of its recorded flora, and possibly a large fraction of its wild fauna, is threatened. Many may be on the verge of extinction. In the last few decades, India has lost at least 50 per cent of its forests; polluted over 70 per cent of its water bodies; built, cultivated or otherwise encroached upon its grasslands; and degraded many coastal areas.

The cheetah and the pink-headed duck are amongst the conspicuous species that have become extinct. More than 150 of the known species of medicinal plants in India have already become extinct due to unsustainable methods of harvesting. Of the species of flora and fauna that remain, over 10 per cent of flowering plants, 21 per cent of mammals and 5 per cent of birds are believed to be under threat. India's domesticated biodiversity is also under threat. Hundreds of crop varieties have disappeared, and even their genes have not been preserved.

Most causes of the loss of biodiversity can be traced, directly or indirectly, to the way we live. Biodiversity is essential for sustainable development, but finding sustainable ways of living is essential for the conservation of biodiversity.

Causes of the Loss of Biodiversity

Biologically diverse natural systems and the services they provide are most often under-valued in monetary terms, and as a result, are used for development activities that seemingly have more direct economic benefits. Large-scale development projects such as industrial plants or hydroelectric projects have contributed substantially to the loss of biodiversity-rich areas. Projects such as the construction of large dams not only result in the submergence of large tracts of forests but also introduce human settlements and roads within forest areas. Between 1951 and 1980, 502,000 hectares of forest were diverted for river valley projects. The enormous demand for minerals in a rapidly industrializing economy has resulted in large-scale deforestation for mining purposes. As many as 70 protected areas, that is, natural areas protected by law and supposed to be free of all destructive human presence, are under threat by ongoing or proposed mining within or adjacent to their borders.

In Goa, nearly 600 mining concessions lie within forest areas rich in biodiversity. Coral reefs, known for their rich biodiversity of marine life, have been exploited for use as raw material in cement manufacture in the country's coastal region.

Large areas rich in biodiversity have been reduced to small pockets due to their conversion to agricultural land or for the construction of roads and housing. Wetlands are filled up to provide space for more housing; large tracts of forests are submerged for hydroelectric projects. This may lead not only to the loss of innumerable species of flora and fauna, but also to the disappearance of entire ecosystems.

Loss of Biodiversity and the Poor

Poverty and Biodiversity day at the IUCN Environment Summit (August 28, 2002) linked the political discussions at WSSD to the realities of rural or poor people and their relationship with natural resources. The majority of the world's poor people continue to live in rural areas and depend heavily on natural ecosystems for their livelihoods. The day's vibrant debates, theatre performance and discussions brought together people from around the world, and from very different situations to share solutions to the global challenge of tackling poverty reduction while maintaining the earth's natural support systems. IUCN shared its strong commitment to supporting governments and civil society in the achievement of the Millennium. Development Goals. A 50 per cent reduction in the number of people living in absolute poverty by 2015 is one of the most urgent milestones in achieving sustainable development, and conservation organizations must join the fight against poverty.

The discussions focused on how conservation could help ensure that biological resources can be positively employed to help the poor secure a sustainable and desirable livelihood. The day brought a broad audience to the Environment Centre, including government delegates. Through these activities and its ongoing programme of work, IUCN aims to increase global understanding of how global policy and natural resource management decisions influence local livelihoods.

Conclusion

1.2 billion people across the globe live with the constant threat of hunger. Among these people, 800 million poor women and men live in rural areas in the developing world. To survive, they use their knowledge and technological and social skills to draw on the natural resources around them to feed themselves and provide other essential goods.

Smallholder agriculture supports the food needs of a large proportion of the world's population.

Farmers are the developers of agricultural biodiversity and are principal managers of terrestrial ecosystems.

Bio-piracy of genetic resources and the privatization of other common property resources such as land and water is on the increase. These resources underpin wealth creation, now more easily captured by industry.

Contamination of Centres of Diversity, international gene banks and the agricultural land-scape by genetically modified organisms is threatening the genetic integrity of the resources that underpin food security. Bio-safety regimes need strengthening with adequate liability obligations.

Trade is taking precedence over sustainable development, equity and the environment. For instance, the concentration of corporate power over the US$ 2 trillion annual food and agriculture trade has increased in recent years through a series of acquisitions and mergers. More than 30 per cent of the global seed market is in the hands of just 10 transnational corporations and just 4 control all GE seeds. These same organizations control most of agricultural research and development spending.

International treaties are often skewed in fovour of corporate interests rather than those of producers and consumers.

Policy support for greater civil society influence in development planning has found little practical foothold in development practice.

Biodiversity can only be conserved and protected by the traditional indigenous knowledge practices of our indigenous communities whose survival and sustenance is intricately linked to biodiversity utilization and conservation. Corporate protectionism in the form of patents and intellectual property rights represents the real threat to democratic rights and economic livelihoods of communities, as well as a source of potential exploitation of the resource base. Biodiversity cannot be privatized by the process of patenting, because biodiversity was not invented by human beings in the first place, therefore can never be privately owned. For achieving this end, there is necessity for policy statements by governments at all levels.

References

Cunningham P., Willium and Barbara W. Saigo, "Environmental Science", 3rd Edition, Wm.C.Brown Publishers, Dubuque, USA, 1995.

Danielle Knight. 'Many Plants in Danger Worldwide', Inter Press Service.

Giles Atkinson, Biodiversity an economic approach, The London School of Economic and Political Science.

ITDG pages on biodiversity at WSSD (2002 World Summit on Sustainable Development).

IUCNN Publications of 2002 (International Union for Conservation of Nature and Natural Resources).

Kiran B., Chhokar, Mamata Pandya, Meena Raghunathan, 'Understanding Economics', sage Publications India private Limited, New Delhi.

KVSG Murali Krishna, 'Glimpses of Environment', Environmental Protection Society, Kakinada.

Laura Carlsen, Indigenous Communities in Latin America: Fighting for Control of Natural Resources in a Globalised Age, Americas Program, (Silver City, NM: Interhemispheric Resource Center).

Part IV: Women Empowerment

By
G. Satyanarayana
M. Reddi Ramu
B. Vijaya Lakshmi
M.V. Raghavulu

20

Promoting Women Entrepreneurship

Introduction

"FREEDOM on economic conditions even more than political the woman is not economically free and self-earning. She will have to depend on her husband or some one else, and dependents are never free. When women move forward, the village moves and the nation moves" **Jawaharlal Nehru (1952)**

Over the last decade, interest in the role of women in economic development has increased greatly. The interest culminated in the launching of the United Nations Women's Decade in 1975. This has resulted in a number of policy recommendations and research priorities promoting the integration of women in development and suggesting ways in which women contribute to this process.

'Entrepreneur' in the current Indian context is an adapter and imitator much more than a true innovator. He is one much more in common with Marshall's organizer of the factors of production rather than Schumpeter's creative disturber.

Women entrepreneur is meant the women or group of women responsible for the existence of a new industrial enterprise. The concept is more akin to Marshall's organizer of the factors of production.

Functions of a Women Entrepreneur: Frederic Harbsion in his article "Entrepreneurial organization as a factor in economic development" specifies the following functions for a women entrepreneur:

1. Explore the prospects of starting new enterprises;
2. The undertaking of risks and the handling of economic uncertainty;
3. Introduction of innovation;
4. Co-ordination, administration and control; and

5. Routine supervision.

Role of Women Entrepreneurship: The countries, which are in the industrialization process, have a congenial climate for women entrepreneurship. These countries are stressing the importance of small scale and cottage industries. These types of industries are very suitable for women.

Women entrepreneurs can generally undertake three types of work:

1. Operate purely as a sub-contractor on raw materials provided by the customer;
2. Manufacture an item to the long-or-short-term order of another enterprises, usually a large scale enterprise; and
3. Manufacture the item for direct sale in the market.

Development of Women Entrepreneurs: Recent Trends: Development of women entrepreneurship should form an internal part of all development efforts. With this view a special study in the seventh Plan has covered the integration of women in economic development. In this regard the plan documents have suggested the following:

1. To treat women as specific target groups in all development programmes;
2. To properly diversity vocational training facilities for women to suit their varied needs and skills;
3. To encourage appropriate technologies, equipment and practice for reducing their efficiency and productivity;
4. To provide marketing assistance the State level; and
5. To increase women's participation in decision-making.

Education and Economic Independence of Women: Rapid transformations are most noticeable in the economic sector, while social changes in general and those concerning the role and status of women in particular lag behind. Economic change may effect women's education and employment, but available research indicates a limited relationship between per capita Gross Product and women's attainment in education and employment.

One of the major recommendations of the New Education Policy of India 1986 is to promote empowerment of women through the agency of education. It is a fact that entrepreneurship is not the special preserve of the educated, but in the case of women already burdened with many social pressures, education is a powerful tool in breaking down the barriers to successful entrepreneurship.

Over the years, the Indian family has undergone a number of changes. The Indian Constitution and statutes, such as, the Hindu Marriage act of 1955 and Hindu Succession Act of 1956 formally gave women a status on par with men. (Dube, 1963, Andre Beteille (1983). These statutory provisions together with urbanization promoted a sort of equalitarian ethos among Indian women particularly among the upper and middle classes who were traditionally deprived access to education and employment.

It is generally held that education and employment of women go a long way for their enjoyment of equality in the social and economic fields and to improve their status (ICSSR, 1975.).

In view of the importance attached to education and employment in improving the economic status of women, it is necessary to examine the significance of aspiration of life of women. Unless one carefully examines these aspects, it is difficult to arrive at solutions and evolve policy prescriptions regarding women's education and employment.

Entrepreneurship among Men and Women: Economic opportunities and incentives are basic for the development of entrepreneurship. Entrepreneurship mainly depends upon individuals and their values, attitudes and personalities. The economists assume that factors of production possess a high degree of mobility; that inputs and outputs are homogeneous and that producers, consumers and resource owners have knowledge of all the possibilities open to them. They emphasize perception of market opportunities as well as operational skills required to run a business or an industry. These include the perception of economic opportunities, technical and organizational skills, managerial competence and motivation to achieve results.

Due to many reasons, entrepreneurship among men is more than women. Most of the women are still engaged with the three

P's- Papads, powder and Pickles, but not to three E's- Electrical, Electronics and Engineering. In the Indian countryside, millions of women are engaged in home production or cottage industries continuing traditional activity and supplementing their family incomes. In the 20th century, the history of India is made notable by the presence of women in large numbers, Shouldering high responsibilities, in the struggle for freedom and in the quest for national reconstruction. As our late Prime Minister Smt. Indira Gandhi said "No society can go ahead if half it is not given opportunity". Men themselves cannot achieve their fullest if there is a large part of the population which is not by their side and helping them. It is in the interest of all that women should be able to play a more positive and more creative role in all spheres nationally and internationally.

Attitude of Government and Society towards Education and Employment of Women: Till 1854, education in India was generally identified with liberal education. Only with woods Dispatch, for the first time, the need for introduction of occupation education was highlighted. The various Committees and Commissions which were appointed to examine the problems of girls' education in India stress the need for making education meaningful and purposeful by gearing it to the social need of our country.

According to M. Chandurkan (1975) "the map of a nation's education, through in a crude form in the beginning, should be made based on the assessed attitudes of the country's women population so as to attain a well designed, attractive and charming figure later on".

Education is the prime and liberal instrument which can develop attitudes, skills for technological sophistication and promote knowledge for economic development. Education and Employment which is conceived to be one of the sure roads to fuller achievement.

Attitude towards women's education and women's employment are considered as very good indicators of women's status in our society. When the attitudes of educated and employed women towards women's education and employment are known, they can be used to predict the present trend and to inculcate the positive attitude towards education and employment.

Women Entrepreneurs and the Need of Science, Technology and Consultancy Services: A major reason for the continued backwardness of the country has been the neglect of human resources resulting out of socio-economic culture. One of the major problems faced in the backward areas is the lack of entrepreneurship. This is all the more so in case of women in whose case, though they represent 50 per cent of world's population and account for two-thirds of the total working hours, they receive about 10 per cent of world's income and own less that 1 per cent of the world's assets. Against this backdrop, women entrepreneurs need special treatment as they belong to the largest disadvantaged group in the country and have to fight against heavy odds. The need for science, technology and consultancy services is treated as most essential especially for women entrepreneurs.

As a result industrialization, urbanization and democratization, the women in India are moving towards emancipation and are seeking gainful employment in various fields. However, the existence of women entrepreneurs in a significant manner is yet to be felt. Women have equal opportunities and rights as men to set up new enterprises. In such a situation, it is essential to identify suitable technology which will enable the women to play her role as an effective entrepreneur without disturbing other priorities. For a women entrepreneur knowledge of science and technology becomes absolutely necessary in this context. This need is not in any way different from the needs of their male counterparts. The essential features of technology in production and other areas, the kind of raw materials required, the method of fabrication, construction, mode of application including the cost of the technology are all important for a women entrepreneur to succeed.

It is often said that entrepreneurs are born not made. But research studies suggest that through proper training, entrepreneurial qualities can be acquired and developed in individuals. The need for providing proper environment for entrepreneurship is of vital importance in the case of women. As such it seems desirable that such qualities may be developed in women entrepreneurs by providing them proper environment and training. This objective can be achieved through proper counseling.

The actual process of entrepreneurial development has three phases. 1. Initiation, 2. Development and 3. Support. Passing through these women can become effective entrepreneurs.

Organisations and Special Schemes in the Service of Women Entrepreneurs: The role of different agencies and organizations towards development of women entrepreneurship in post-independent India, how they provide different kinds of entrepreneurial skills and facilities to the women entrepreneurs were unfortunately deprived of such facilities as there were no organizations to come to their help. But in the gradual course of time, different agencies and organization which have come into being, not only provide the financial assistance but also provide proper training in the science and art of entrepreneurship, technological know-how and consultancy services.

In other words it may be said that the organizations and agencies are just like the lubricating oil to run the machinery of entrepreneurship. If an entrepreneur is the captain of the ship of the enterprise, the organizations and agencies which come to the help of entrepreneurs are like steering wheels of the ship.

With the advance of science and technology, a certain amount of change has come about. An increasing number of women are wanting to participate in the economic activities of the nation. Thus we find the emergence of women entrepreneurs. A women entrepreneur is a person who is an enterprising individual with an eye for opportunities, and an uncanny vision, commercial acumen, with tremendous perseverance and above all a person who is willing to take risks with the unknown because of the adventurous spirit they possess.

Classification of Women Entrepreneurs

According to Samuel and Johnson 91087), women who become entrepreneurs may be classified into five categories:

1. Those who become entrepreneurs due to economic needs;
2. Those who take it as a challenge to satisfy some of their personality needs i.e., power, achievement, novel experience etc;
3. those who would take it up as a leisure time activity;
4. Those who would like to utilize the knowledge gained; and
5. Those who take it up as a family occupation.

Women entrepreneurs can also be classified into three categories on the basis of the nature of the industry that they set up. They are as follows:

Entrepreneurs in Large and Medium Sectors: In large and medium sectors women with educational and professional qualifications take the initiatives and manage the business as well as a man. A women entrepreneur who has received basic managerial training and educational qualifications, sometimes even an MBA degree, usually may take up employment in medium sector and large units. These women, because of their qualifications and other opportunities which are available to them, are in a superior position and have a competitive edge over others to set up and manage the units.

Entrepreneurs in the Small Sector: Those women entrepreneurs who do not have education or any formal training in management, but have developed skills take to small scale industry. They choose that product with which they are familiar i.e., garments weaving, pickles, dolls and handicrafts. Some have ventured into engineering, electronics, chemicals and pharmaceuticals. Some also make surgical instruments, furniture and property.

Entrepreneurs in the Service Sector: The third category of women entrepreneurs work in cities and slums to help men who have lower means of livelihood. They are in service oriented organizations to help economically backward sections. They need government support in marketing as well as getting finance at a concessional rate of interest. Preferential purchasing policy of Government helps such institutions to manufacture and sell items like files, chalk, stationary etc.

Women in our country have always been the victims of neglect and discrimination and were not allowed to perform their due role in the economic or social life of the society. Recognising the injustice meted out to women in the past, our constitution took special care to guarantee equal rights and opportunities for both men and women in political, economical and social fields and to specially prohibit any discrimination particularly in matters of employment wages and humane conditions of work.

Conclusion

Inspite of forming 50 per cent of the total population of the world, women do not even possess one per cent of the world's property. Their role and contribution in industrialization has remained unaccounted and unassessed. Time has come for women to come out of the drudgery of housework and give vent to their creativity and entrepreneurship. The specific role of women in the economic effort has not yet been particularly felt by women themselves. With the increase in the number of women getting self employed, the role and status of women is also bound to change gradually in the society. It is heartening that women have excelled themselves in all branches of human activity in the modern age of globalisation. The Governments all over the world need to recognize and tap the potentials of the women for economic development for the real development takes place only when the women develops in all fields.

References

Agarwal, G. K., "Empowerment of Women through Rural Industrialization-An Indian Experiences", National Bank News Review, Jan-March, 1997.

Batra, N.D. "Why this Growing Agro Cities on women", Jojana (1988), Vol. 32, No. 9.

Bindra "Social studies entrepreneurship with Energy Conservation", New Heights Publishers & Distributors, New Delhi.

Desai, Vasant Profile of a women entrepreneur, Entrepreneurial Development, Himalaya Publishing House, Mumbai.

Deshpande, Entrepreneurship of small Scale Industries, Deep Manohar, V. and Deep Publishers, New Delhi.

Gupta, C.B., Entrepreneurship Development in India,

Jasmer Singh Saini "Entrepreneurship development programmes and Practices", Deep and Deep Publications, New Delhi.

Manohar, K.M. Women status and Development Programmes in India, Society for women's Studies and Development, Warangal.

Sami Uddin "Entrepreneurial Development in India", Mittal Mehfoozur Rehman Publications New Delhi

Sivakami, A. Micro Profile of Women Entrepreneurs, M. Sc. Dissertation, Queen Marry College, Madras.

21

Role of Women in Rural Development

Introduction

It is a widely accepted opinion that development in the case of developing countries like India implies in progressive withdrawal of workers engaged in agricultural activities. Because agriculture is over burdened with more than 65 per cent of the people eking out their livelihood from agriculture in India. One is surprised at the skewed distribution of wealth and landed property in India. It is a bitter truth that the top 20 per cent of the people have command over 80 per cent resources, including land in India. Perhaps it is a because of this reason poverty continued to be unsolved problem in India. Intensity of poverty is felt more in rural India and women are the worst affected victims of poverty in rural areas. This article examines the role of women-headed-households (WHHs) in rural development in Anantapur district. Women headed households refer to those households that are being managed and maintained by women who have assumed the role of head of the households. The women who head the households who are either windows that have lost their husbands or those whose husbands have became too weak to head the households and in our study, the former constitutes 45 per cent and the latter 55 per cent of the sampled households. As rural social change is eagerly anticipated through development efforts the role played by women is grudgingly acknowledged. But before long, how are they influenced, it is by institutional agencies or through their own urban contacts will be very interesting to note. This paper examines all these aspects as mentioned earlier.

Sample Area and Respondents

Two villages viz., Akuthotapalli and Itikalapalli in Anantapur rural Mandals of Anantapur district, each with more than 600 households formed the study area.

The villages are selected in random. These two villages are being located on either side of the Sri Krishnadevaraya University Campus and are within a radius of 10 kms. from Anantapur district headquarters.

However, Anantapur rural Mandals was chosen in view of its socio-economic characteristic which is worth studying as most of the rural development programmes are vigorously implemented in this mandal in Anantapur District.

The data relating to 200 women respondents from both the sampled villages were pooled together for the purpose of analysis and presentation. The respondents were purposively selected in order to give due representation to all the vulnerable castes in the study area. The number of households studied on the basis of cast were Kuraba (55 households), Gollas (35 households), Boyas (28 households), Potters (25 households), SC's (30 households), ST's (20 households), Lingayats (7 households). Those households were selected in proportion to their total population in the villages.

Socio-Economic Characteristics of the Sample Respondents

The same respondents: Kurabas, Gollas, Boyas, Lingayats and Potters own land in the pattern of 7.5, 7.2, 5.0, 3.9 and 1.8 acres respectively as the caste order presented above and it is significant to note that both SC's and ST's are the landless villagers who solely depended on their labour for livelihood.

As regards to education, 162 respondents (81 per cent) were literates, only 32 respondents (18.5 per cent) illiterates who did not even attend night schools. The family literacy level for females was 37 per cent while it was above 62 per cent for males in the sample households. The household were engaged in varied occupations, such as, agriculture and allied activities; self-employment-basket weaving, silk weaving, stone-breaking, road laying works, petty shops, tailoring, dairying and vegetables, fruits vending, brick lying, house construction works, food grain processing and domestic servants.

The urban contact by the village men had another repercussion on the family income. Men inclined to reduce their contribution to the family income as they were spending substantial amount of their earnings on liquor and eating out. This has resulted in less income to the household and many women bitterly complained about this practice. This practice also led to frequent bickerings in the family, especially, among the lower income households that we have taken for our study.

Another interesting dimension of urban contact by the rural women has led to a through in their attitude towards work. Many of the women in the sample villages (Akuthotapalli and Itikalapalli), who were educated up to primary and secondary levels were now looking down upon their family occupation-agriculture. Gone were the days when they would pursue this occupation with devotion and now most of them were hoping against hope of pursuing gainful employment which would fetch them good income to sustain them. Besides, some of them eagerly migrated to the near by cities and remained non-communicant to their parents. This has added on increased burden on the women in the households in terms of household and farm work.

It may be seen in Table 21.1 that the sampled households engaged in agriculture and allied activities to earn livelihood. Although the two villages located nearby the district urban centre, self-employment, ventures attempted by the sampled women headed households are depressing as it is only three per cent of them took up self-employment avenues.

It is significant to notice that 30 per cent of the households find these employments in stone breaking and road lying and house construction works. These activities provide work almost throughout the year (Table 21.1).

Anantapur is basically fruits and vegetables growing area, the transportation of which gave raise a good demand for basket manufacturing sectors. Here again women find employment during major part of the year. Similarly, women have been engaged throughout the year in silk handloom weaving and few of them in tailoring works.

Table 21.1: Occupational Distribution of the Sampled Households

S. No	Type of Activity	Percentage
1.	Agriculture labours	20
2.	Dairying	15
3.	Vegetables and Fruits vending	10
4.	Self-employment (Petty Business)	3
5.	Stone breaking and Road lying works	10
6.	Household activities (Basket weaving, silk handloom weaving, tailoring)	15
7.	Brick laying	5
8.	House construction	15
9.	Food grain processing (free food)	2
10.	Domestic servants (free food)	5
Total		100

Source: Field Survey.

As mentioned earlier the villages located on either side of Sri Krishnadevaraya University campus women find work either as domestic servants or food grains processing workers in the Sri Krishnadevaraya University campus. Income earned by women workers in other than agriculture sector seemed to be encouraging. As seen from the Table 21.2 an agriculture labourer gets Rs. 50 as a daily wage as against Rs. 70 in vegetables and fruits vending, Rs. 70 in stone breaking and road laying works; Rs.60 as a construction worker and Rs.80 as a worker in household activities.

The annual incomes of the women headed households is the highest in the case of dairying activities Rs. 57,600 followed by household activities, self-employment, stone breaking and road laying works, brick laying and house construction works, vide Table 21.2.

Income earned through self-employment activities is quite

encouraging. There is a lot of scope for women to exploit and to enrich themselves in these activities in the villages.

Table 21.2: Annual Income of the Sampled Households (Rs.)

S. No	Type of Activity	Daily Earning of a Worker	No. of Workers per Household	No. of Working days in a year	Annual Income of the Households
1.	Agriculture labours	50	2	180	18,000
2.	Dairying	80	2	360	57,600
3.	Vegetables & Fruits vending	70	1	240	16,800
4.	Self-employment	100	1	360	36,000
5.	Stone breaking and Road lying works	70	3	240	33,600
6.	Household activities (Basket weaving etc.)	50	3	360	54,000
7.	Brick laying	60	2	180	21,600
8.	House construction	60	3	200	36,000
9.	Food grain processing (free food)	30	3	240	21,600
10.	Domestic servants (free food)	15	3	360	16,200

Source: field survey data.

The illiterate and hard working women who belonged to traditional house construction community-Vadderlu, finding work throughout the year because there are half a dozen stone crushing & quarries units within a distance of 4 Kms. from these two villages.

In the case of women who are engaged in food grain processing work, and domestic works of course, have been getting the lowest annual income per house hold. This is, as reported, they were served free food on all the working days; and in addition they would provide used clothes; hence the wages were lower compared to the wages of workers engaged in other sectors in the villages. It is mostly SC's and ST's women that taken these two category of works in the villages.

Contact with Institutional Agencies

The most important source of knowledge regarding agriculture an allied activities for the rural people is imparted through the contact with the institutional agencies, such as, Agricultural Extension Officers, Veterinary Doctors, Health Works, Gram Sevak etc. They provided them with recent information about the innovations in agricultural, subsidiary occupation, the schemes of rural credit, advice on health problems.

The lack of contact with extension agencies was the reason for many rural women losing touch with technological innovations. The next frequent visit was made by; the gram sevak and community health workers situated within easy teach of people, they made cursory visit as they were forced to show their diaries to their superiors. The lowest numbers of contacts were made by the Agriculture Extension Officer. It may be mentioned here that the knowledge level of participants regarding the high yielding varieties, pesticides, etc. was not an appreciative level. This is mainly because of the neglect of women in the dissemination of knowledge of farm practices.

The most un-cherished contact official for the rural people was the contact with the Agricultural Bank Officer. The felt that the official was not sympathetic toward their problem in repayment of loans and through that they visited them to rob their little possession even, as they; were unable to repay the loan amount for one or the other reasons,

The above discussion indicates a wrong identification of the problems and needs of the rural women while trying to help them in their needs. Therefore increased attention to the extension needs of rural women must be paid through the services of the women extension officers. Most of the women expressed that it was especially incompatible for him of freely mix with the male extension agencies.

The extension agencies should take special interest to give importance to the extension needs of the women who have taken up the dairying and silk handloom weaving as a part of rural development schemes.

The neglect of women in developing countries regarding to dissemination of extension knowledge in agronomic research is not uncommon. It is observed that in the study, WHHs who have taken up agriculture have been using traditional methodology of cultivation. Hence, appropriate technology has to be developed and passed on to actual cultivators, so that that they may enhance their productivity levels in the rural areas.

Urban Contact of Respondents

Owing the nearness to the urban centre of Anantapur has some effect on the knowledge level and the attitude of women respondents in the villages. The frequent interaction with Agriculture Extension Officer, Veterinary doctor, state bank of India Agricultural Field officer, Ananta Grameena Bank Field Officer, community health workers and primary health centre doctors in the S.K.University campus and panchayat Extension Officers have richly helped the households to acquaint themselves with the necessary knowledge and service to improve their economic well-being in the study area.

The respondents seek more of the services of bankers, agricultural Extension officers, veterinary doctors and community health workers to increase their efficiency levels in the works that they have taken up of their works.

It is heartening to note that more number of women workers engaged in sectors other than agriculture. More number of women has been engaged in activities, such as, dairying, basket weaving, silk handloom weaving, vegetables and fruits vending the house construction than in agricultural sector. As such the women have an opportunity to mix with the outside world, which may help in breaking caste division through marketing their commodities.

Of late, the number of Auto rickshaws has increased in their number and for every ten minutes one Auto rickshaw of either seven seater or three seater would be plying between these villages and Anantapur town facilitating the villages either to buy or sell goods at Anantapur urban centre.

Conclusion

On the whole, the services rendered by Anantapur Urban Centre and institutional contact of the rural WHH respondents seemed to be encouraging in improving their living conditions. Most of the WHHs have complained that they did have access to bank finances as they lack the required knowledge and their inability to produce co-obligates in availing themselves of bank loans to take up some enterprises, which have a lot of potentials in villages. A few of the WHHs could effectively check their husbands' indulgence in drinking and gambling habits which improved the saving levels the ploughing back of these savings may result in income-yielding assets among the sampled WHHs and if this trend continued vigorously for a considerable period it finally ends up in rural development in the study area.

References

A.W. Lewis, (1972), "The Theory of Economic Growth", George Allen & Unwin Ltd., London.

Anand Sarup, (1990), "Planning for the Millions (promise & Performance)", wiley Eastern Limited, New Delhi.

Geraldine Forbes, (1998), "Women in Modern India", Cambridge University press, New Delhi.

K. Venkata Reddy, (2001), "Agriculture and Rural Development (A Gandhian Perspective)", Himalaya Publishing house, Mumbai.

Satish Kumar, (1982), "The Schumcher Lectures", abacus edition published, London.

22

Role of Women: Problems and Solutions

Introduction

Women hold half the sky as such they cannot be ignored in the nation building and their active participation in the economic development, especially, in the context of a developing country, like India.

If one observes recent trends one unfailingly comes to a conclusion that women compete equally with their men folk in every activity, including Software sector, Industry, Administration, Judiciary, Participation political activities and space excavation ventures. With every Sun rise one is witnessing ever increasing in number of women in diverse activities and apart from performing assigned duties as mothers and wives at home. Their active involvement in the diverse sectors of the country has empowered them rendering to improve their stand of living.

It is a widely accepted opinion that development in the case of developing countries like India implies progressive withdrawal of workers engaged in agricultural activities. Because agriculture is over burdened with more than 65 per cent of the people eking out their livelihood from agriculture in India. One is surprised at the skewed distribution of wealth and landed property in India.

It is a better truth that the top 20 per cent of the people have command over 80 per cent resources, including land in India. Perhaps it is a because of this reason poverty continued to be unsolved problem in India. Intensity of poverty is felt more in rural India and women are the worst affected victims of poverty in rural areas. Women headed households refer to those households that are being managed and maintained by women who have the role of head of the households. The women who head the households who are either widows that have lost their husbands or those whose husbands have become too weak to head the households and in our study, the former constitutes 45 per cent and the later 55 per cent of the sampled households. As rural social change is eagerly anticipated through development efforts he role played by women is grudgingly acknowledged. But before long, how are they influenced, it is by institutional agencies or through their own urban contacts will be very interesting to note.

Empowerment of women has emerged as one the major issues of development after the International Conference on population and development at Cairo and women's conference at Beijing and gender equality has been considered as one of the essential components of human development in recent years. Gender disparity varies among countries depending upon the socio-economic context, which prevails significantly in the SAARC (South Asian Association for Regional Cooperation) region due to the limited efforts of the countries-Bangladesh, Bhutan, India, Maldives, Nepal, Pakistan and Sri Lanka-to equalize the opportunities between males and females. The patriarchal societies of SAARC countries have been influenced by the feudal culture and the age-old image of women keeps her illiterate, economically unorganized, socially inferior and legally helpless and their image in public life have been negatively influenced due to their unvalued and under valued work in economic terms. Although a modest socio-economic growth was visible in the SAARC countries in the last decade, the problem of gender disparity remains persisting, besides poverty.

Despite the fact that empowering women through investing in their capabilities makes greater strides in the economic growth and the overall development of the countries, these governments have not made any serious efforts towards women's upliftment. However, in the recent past, there has been a positive move-a slow change in the mental attitudes and awareness of the economic activity rates of females-in the societies and governments of the region. They have started recognizing the importance of encouraging the importance of encouraging women to acquire economic opportunities and even establishing some departments in the governments for their progress. Along the sidelines, non-government organizations (NGOs) are also striving vigorously for women's cause especially in the rural sector in these societies. Viewed against this background, this paper aims at increasing the attention drawn in favour of the economic empowerment of women in the SAARC countries and also highlights the need for gender-focused policies and makes a case for a greater social investment in women.

Status of Women

In the SAARC, region women are continuously relegated to a secondary position as they live and work under disadvantaged conditions due to the predominantly agrarian structure of these economies. The problems facing women in these countries are enormous-viz., low levels of literacy, poor enrolment in schools coupled with high drop outs, lack of vocational and technical training, marketing and credit facilities, low health and nutritional status, low economic activity rates, poor political participation and less involvement in policy making apart from the prevailing customs, traditions and social taboos, as shown in the following Table 22.1 presents the female disparity in health and literacy fields and the share of females in the total labour force.

An overall improvement in life expectancy at birth was registered in these countries from 1985 to 1998 in both males and females. Though female life expectancy was higher than males in the later year with the exception of Maldives, the life expectancy in the former year was lower in females till recently, defying the fact that women five longer than man due to biological norms reflecting the low nutritional status and the inadequate health facilities available to them. There was a wide, variation between Sri Lanka women and the rest in SAARC owing to the proper extension of health services to the people on the former particularly in rural areas. This country has a better quality of life in the entire developing world even when its income levels are lower. Adult literacy of females was also substantially low in the SAARC countries barring Sri Lanka and Maldives, despite its

Table 22.1: SAARC: Women in Development

Country	Life Expectancy at Birth				Adult Literacy Rate (% of people 15 and above)				Female labour force (% of total labour force)	
	1985		1998		1990		1998		1980	1999
	Female	Male	Female	Male	Female	Male	Female	Male		
Bangladesh	50	51	59	58	22	47	29	51	42	42
Bhutan	-	-	63	60	-	-	-	-	-	-
India	56	57	64	62	34	62	43	67	34	32
Maldives	-	-	64	66	34	-	96	96	-	-
Nepal	46	47	58	58	13	38	22	57	39	40
Pakistan	50	52	63	61	21	47	29	58	23	28
Sri Lanka	72	68	76	71	83	93	88	94	27	36

Source: World Bank, World Development Report, various years, Oxford Press, New York.

significant contribution to the decline in infant mortality, high acceptance of family welfare, fertility decline, delayed age at marriage, better hygienic conditions and above all women's status in society.

The female literacy was less than half of male literacy-through both were at low levels-in Bangladesh, Nepal, and Pakistan and was a little over half in India in 1990. Notwithstanding the considerable improvement in the female literacy from 1990 to 1998, the female gap was still high in these countries including India. Sri Lanka with least gender disparity and Maldives, with gender quality in adult literacy stand as better examples not only in the SAARC region but also in the entire Asia. Low labour participation rates of females in the region reflect the lack of education and training along with the socio-cultural factors that restrict the entry of women into labour market. A modest increase in the female labour force was noticed only in Sri Lanka and Pakistan from 1980 to 1999. The relatively high rates in Bangladesh and Nepal were attributed to the significant proportion of women in agriculture and allied activities. Interestingly, the rate India witnessed a slowing down from 1980 to 1999 perhaps due to the problems of enumeration.

An attempt has been made to identify the problems of rural women and prescribe suggestive measures to solve them.

In the civilization all over the world the status and condition of women has seen ups and downs, more of downs and less of ups. Society is never static, however the path of equality for women, is a story full of injustice. The role of the women in the first wave civilization may seem like a backward one, but infect it was much more evenly balanced between the sexes than what it is today. During the initial stages of human evolution when men worked mainly as hunters and women as gatherers of other food. Thus women enjoyed a large clout as they were the major collectors of the food.

However, the second wave civilization that is the industrial civilization brought changes in the social sphere along with changes in the economical sphere. It brought radically new forms of social organization. It brought in new and varied forms of families. When men and women left the farmers, for the factories the equality, that is the equitable division of power, got titled in the favour of the men. In all the fields of activities the politics, the Arts, the education, the business and in other fields. Men started domination and women were driven back to the kitchen. Even when they worked wages were kept to the minimum and chances of their controlling levels of power and management were minimized. Simultaneously control over the income was absolutely denied.

In today's scenario the First world is moving into the third wave and the socio sphere is once again on the move, slowly the third wave technology is bringing the production to home. As this trend grows women are occupying more equitable position or atleast the doors of the opportunities for sharing power are opening bit by bit.

However, our country still remains confined to socio sphere introduced and sustained by industrialization. The women are excluded from even a nodding acquaintance with higher fields of activities, be they philosophical, be they theological be they political, be they economical, or be they sociological. Ideologically we want to be in the first wave civilization; materially we are planning for industrialization with our eye towards the third wave technology, while we continue to continue women to the lowly place in the social hierarchy!

Throughout the middle ages our society confined women to purdha and four walls of their home. While Gandhi and his struggle enabled women to take a true breath and participate in his activities, still the overall status of women has remained low. Even in the households where women are the sole income earners (about 18.7 per cent of household in India). Accordingly to M.S. Swaminathan women are the sole or chief bread winner in 25 per cent of the poverty sticken families, their status remains low.

It can be noticed that among the working population proportion of women on an average is about $1/3^{rd}$. Most of them are employed in the areas of activities with lesser income and harder work such as marginal farmers and agricultural labourers. In agricultural labourers women are employed in predominant numbers from the figures. Both in Gujarat and Kheda Dist. The percentage is much larger.

However, these indicators are based on activities which generate income. Household work, child rearing etc. which form the major burden of women's work is not at all reflected in the study.

According to the census commissioner Mr. J.K. Bantia, it is heartening to note the gap between male and female literacy has narrowed down during 1991-2001.

The special difficulty that women work force is extraordinary work burden or lack of access to health care and other social welfare measures. These difficulties are rooted in the sexual division of labour, marked by a double work burden, (at home and outside) and by specific nature of tasks they do and in the unequal distribution of resources like food within the household, which stems from women's inferior status in household and from a lack of control over cash and productive resources like land.

The problems of women belonging to better off sections in rural area are more or less similar to those of urban women. However, they are more intensified due to more conservative and confining social mores of rural society. However, poor rural women have to face additional problems due to their struggle for there existence and getting minimum requirement for survival.

The major issues they face can be listed as.

- Shortage of fuel, fodder and water.
- Problems of nutrition and health including sanitation.
- Unequal income distribution and sexual exploitation in work places.
- Lack of control over earnings.
- Unequality of status between genders.

As indicated in Table 22.2 for rural women every dawn brings with it a long march in search of fuel, fodder and water. It does not matter if the women are old, young or pregnant. Caught between poverty and environmental destruction, poor rural women in India could well be reaching the limits of physical endurance. Thus for collecting fuel and fodder and fetching water women have to spend several hours a day. In the border areas of Gujarat they have to spend six to nine hours a day for collecting firewood. Moreover landlessness adds to the problems of collecting both fodder and firewood for poor women. They don't have their own sources. This problem is more acute as the comparatively better all farmers have started using their resources fully. They have nothing to space for the landless poor.

Table 22.2: Time Spent by Women on Household Activities in Different Parts of India (Hours/Days)

Particulars of the Places	Hours/Day
Fetching water Eastern Up	1.0-3.9
Western up (pregnant women)	0.8-3.0
Karnataka	1.0-1.4
Fuel Wood gathering	-
Himalayan	4.0-7.2
Karnataka	0.4-0.9
Fetching water & Fuel Wood gathering	-
Gujarat-Rajasthan border	6.0-9.0
Grazing Animals	-
Western Up (pregnant women)	0-3.0
Karnataka	0.5-1.0
Making Dung Cakes	-
Western Up (pregnant Women)	0-0.5

Source: Government of India Statistical Data, Hyderabad.

The story of poor landless women in character tract of Kheda district is typical. In anand taluka especially the cash crops are very important hence fodder is considered the least important crop. Naturally with no fodder access to local firewood and fodder the poor women have to lament "while we don't have enough money for food from where are we to get firewood?" This problem is further aggravated due to inefficient chullas giving out harmful smoke and consuming more fuel.

On average the source of water is about 1.5 kms. away fetching the water sufficient for the households becomes a strenuous activity and women have to spend long hours for that.

Women get much less food than required. This leaves them ill-nourished. Which in turn makes them prone to sickness. Repeated child bearing have major negative effect on their health. Prevailing social norms and struggle for dry today living prevent them from seeking medical care even during pregnancy or serious sickness. In the prevailing conditions of perpetual scarcity women are forced to look for work on relief projects such as food for work however the little food or money they earn benefits them the last.

According to Batliwala the amount of energy spent by women is about 2,505 calories daily and by men 2473 calories, but when food intake is compared men get nearly 800 calories more than what they expend, while women get 100 calories less. During pregnancy and lactation women need an extra 500 calories to 600 calories a day. At any point in time, one third of the women in the country are in this condition, but most of them continue to wok without any additional nutrition. The woman is the last to get food in an India household.

Survey shows that women are not able to avail of health care to the same extent as the men. As per study by IIM A 'bad the sex ration of patients at a public health center was 5 per cent in favour of men.

The discriminating attitude toward the Female child in the society results in higher infant mortality rate which will be evident from the Table (22.2a).

According to the population policy it is targeted to reduce infant mortality rate below 30 per 1000 live births and maternal mortality rate below 100 per 1 lakh live births.

Coupled with this cultural & traditional shyness in reporting illness are major factors. The long working hours of women do not leave them with enough time to go to health centers which in any case are far away inadequately staffed equipped.

Table: 22.2(a) Infant Mortality Rate

Year	Number of deaths per 1000 persons.	
	Male	Female
1972	132	148
1980	113	115
1981	108	170

Source: Census of population Report, 1981.

All these factors collectively contribute to lower life expectancy among women as shown in the Table (22.2b).

Table: 22.2(b) Expectation of Life at Birth

Period	Male	Female
1951-61	41.91	40.6
1961-71	46.4	44.7
1971-81	54.1	54.7
2001	63.9	66.9

Source: Census of population Report, 2001.

Maternal mortality is a major cause of higher death rate in women. The pregnant women and recent mothers receive no or scant attention either from families or from physicians.

Even during child caring stage rural women are required to work same 15 or 16 long hours a day. Further no guidance regarding pre or post natal care is available. For child bearing maternity homes are out of question but even scientifically trained nursing services just do not exist in most of the villages. Work burden of rural women leaves them no time for the child care. The poor babies with below average birth weight receive neither the care nor the nourishment. This results in high infant mortality and especially if the baby is the girl child.

Apart from traditional occupational health problems which women workers share with their made counter parts they suffer from additional disadvantage. Women are required to look after their young ones, yet there is no provision in most of the cases for child care at the place of work is it in the form or in factory. As a result the child has to be left in care of a little or older sibling or has to be carried to the work place and left unattended for long durations. This anxiety and tension tells upon the general health & further aggravate the problem of malnourished mothers.

Having had a look at the problems of the women a few prescriptions are suggested below of course awareness and organizing for equality are of prime importance. A few specific activities which can be undertaken are also suggested.

1. Public campaigns and mass context both through print and non print Medias as well as mobilization through personal contact should be launched. This campaign should aim at creating awareness about women's rights and enable them to organize to light against suppression and exploitation and to demand their rights. The print media used for this purpose should be in simple regional language.
2. A large numbers of women extension workers should be deployed in the villages. Their role will be to impact information regarding government schemes and programmes beneficial to women. They should actively assist in training women, forming their cooperatives etc. So that real benefit accrues to women.
3. Mass base organized efforts should be promoted and encouraged to get fair deal for the rural poor women.
4. Mahila Samitis and Mahila Mandals should be established, nurtured and made active. For this purpose NGOs at grass root level and Govt. functionaries will have to extend their help. They can lead them towards sharing of power structure with an aim that women targeted agricultural development programmes are offered. Women producers should be enabled to get inputs such as subsidies, fertilizers, improved seeds etc. They should be further supported for storing and marketing their produce.
5. In introduction of new technologies for alleviation of drudgery of women's household work their participation

should be assured through organized efforts to make the technology really effective and useful.

6. Assurance of essential commodities at affordable prices should be the priority area. If need be under the social welfare policies of the state subsidies also should be provided. These essential commodities include potable water, fodder fuel apart from the cereals.
7. Since fuel is topmost priority the social forestry programme of the government should be oriented towards fuel producing fuel naturally this will have to be of multi-cropping pattern so that fuel the available are the year around. Further mechanisms will have to be involved to see that equitable distribution of the yield of social forestry programme is ensured and rural poor are not deprived of the legitimate needs.
8. Women labour should be diversified by introduction of horticulture, food processing, vegetable growing etc. to ensure sustained long term employment instead of seasonal employment as at present.
9. Organizations and individuals should be identified so that necessary technical and manageable support reaches out to the rural poor women for plant rearing, maintenance and protection.
10. Agriculture policy and programmes should be designed taking into consideration women's contribution to agriculture. Adequate resources should be allocated to such programmes and the implementation should be women oriented.
11. Agro-based co-operatives should launch a drive for enrolling women members, if need be or providing reservation to assure women's role in decision making.
12. The surplus land should be distributed to women in case of women headed families. In other cases also their equal ownership should be assured.
13. Health, child rearing and nutrition services should be provided to each village programmes should be devised to pay special attention to pregnant and lactating women as well

as old and incapacited women.

14. Proper health and safely standards to be ensured at all work places for women. Provision of cruches where needed should be also made.
15. Sanitary latrines, should be provided as far as possible for individuals household so that women do not suffer from myriad health problems due to lack of privacy.
16. Alcohol shops should be banned through strict enforcement of Law.
17. Research should be encouraged to develop technologies and tools to reduce the drudgery of the work. The tools should be simple and easily adoptable. However, care should be taken that the introduction of the technology does not result into displacement of women from employment.
18. Innovations in existing technologies tools exclusively used by women such as cashew nuts processing, sewing machines etc. Should be introduced by considering anthropology of Indian women at present most of the technologies are based on physiology of western women or that of the man.
19. Suitable extension network should be established for dissemination of information regarding technology to reach the correct groups of women without much procedural delays.
20. Training in the skill & necessary for the activities listed earlier should be organized on regular basis. Appropriate facilities for literacy and liberal and general education should be evolved. Such training and education should be preferably imported by women trainees.
21. Law enforcement agencies should se that fair wages are given to women without gender discrimination.
22. Mahila banks managed by women to support women's economic activity on liberal terms should be established Borrowing by proxy be man in name of women should be discouraged.

References

A.W. Lewis, (1972), "The Theory of Economic Growth", George Allen & Unwin Ltd., London.

K. Venkata Reddy, (2001), "Agriculture and Rural Development (A Gandhian Perspective)", Himalaya Publishing House, Mumbai.

Satish Kumar, (1982), "The Schumcher Lectures", abacus edition published, London.

Dr. Amarapali, M. "Journal Nirnay", Sardar Patel Institute of Public Administration, Govt. of Gujarat, Ahmedabad.

Anand Sarup, (1990), "Planning for the Millions (promise & Performance)", Wiley Eastern Limited, New Delhi.

Geraldine Forbes, (1998), "Women in Modern India", Cambridge University press, New Delhi.

7. Batra, N.D. "Why this Growing Agro Cities on women", Jojana (1988), Vol. 32, No.9.
8. Deshpande, Manohar, V. Entrepreneurship of small Scale Industries, Deep and Deep Publishers, New Delhi.
9. Desai, Vasant, Profile of a women entrepreneur, Entrepreneurial Development, Himalaya Publishing House, New Delhi.

Part V: Tourism and Economic Development

By
G. Satyanarayana
M. Reddi Ramu
M.V. Raghavulu

23

Sustainable Tourism: A Case Study of Chittoor District

Introduction

Tourism is one of the fastest growing industries in the world today. It creates employment especially for guides, restaurants, hoteliers, local shopkeepers, merchants etc. and brings in foreign currency to economically marginal areas. And also it plays an important role in the social culture and economic development of the nations, and has the potential to preserve the heritage. Tourism is not only a major social phenomenon of the modern society with enormous economic consequences but also the world's largest export industry, which accounts for about 8 per cent of the total world's largest export more than 30 per cent of the international trade in services, 10.7 per cent of the global work force and about 12 per cent of world GDP.

India is a centre for two primitive civilizations of the world. One is the Indus valley civilizations and the Aryan civilization. The republic of India is the Sixth largest country in the world preceded by China, Canada, Brazil, the United States of America and Australia. Tourism development in this country has been started in the early Sixties. By that time, all other countries have achieved a remarkable progress in this area and has exploited to a maximum possible extent. India declared as industry in 1988 and as a Year of Tourism in 1991. According to the annual report of Ministry of Tourism and Civil Aviation for 1977-78, India's Gross Foreign Exchange earning from tourism was Rs. 283 crore. When the country received 19.9 per cent more tourists than in the previous year in India. Share still only about one per cent of the world's total tourist trade.

Tourism thus, grew on its own and, from 15,000 tourists in 1950, reached a figure of 2.98 Millions arrivals in the year 2004 (up to November). However, the rate of international arrivals in India in recent years has been to the tune of about 19 lakh arrivals per year. The un-precedented growth in tourism in India has made in the third largest foreign exchange earner after gems and Jewellery and ready-made garments. This is not surprising since India possesses a whole range of attractive normally sought by tourists and which includes natural attractions like landscapes, Scenic beauty, Mountains, Wildlife, Beaches, Major Rivers and made attractions such as Mountains, Forts, Palaces and hovels. Hence, with all these, the main source of market for India are United Kingdom and the United States followed by Sri-Lanka, France, Germany, Canada, Japan, Australia, and Singapore.

Concept of Sustainable Tourism

Sustainable tourism is led by motives like spirit of enquiry, love of beauty, search for knowledge and respect for nature. It aims at quality tourism, which creates the least damage to the natural, social, cultural environment. If proper sewage disposal system has not been installed for hotel, or other tourist boarding points the groundwater may get polluted from the sewage. Owing to excessive use of internal combustion vehicles such as cars and buses used by tourists in particular area exates air pollution. Noise generated by the concentration of tourists, tourists vehicles and sometimes by certain types of tourist attraction such amusement parts may reach uncomfortable and irritating levels for residents of the area resulting in sound pollution. Over use or misuse of environmentally fragile archaeological and historical sites can led to damage of this feature through excessive wear, vibration and vandalism (Butler, R.W. 1990).

Tourism has become a major and an integral part of economic, social and physical development. It comprises complete system of nature, the universe, the space and the galaxy, which includes the man and his activities, wild life, mountains and valleys, rivers and waterfalls forests and trees, social and cultural system, flora and fauna, the sea. Now tourism has become means of employment generation for a country. Tourist's point of view tourism makes dreams of sight seeing, experience, know about the historical accounts, means of hobby etc. However, the flow of tourists to different places of country consists of important components of eco-systems. This includes hill stations, seacoasts, rivers, lakes, waterfalls etc. The tourism connected with these eco-systems often viewed with understanding of that environment and its conservation and also keeping eco-health (sanitation of the environment).

Factors Promoting Sustainable Tourism

The Sustainable Tourism hinges upon the 'overall management' as a viable method in sustainable tourist activities. The overall quality approach renders the management of products especially of tourist areas, extremely sensitive to the preferences and expectations of consumers. The private public profitability of a tourist destination will depend on the client's sanitation, since they will return more often and stay longer and will transmit a positive image of their holiday experiences to others. Insofar as these preferences and expectations include the demand for unspoilt settings and consumer satisfaction, the profitability of a tourist spot, will call for the development of strategies for sustainable development.

One can believe this is a productive approach for sustainability in the tourist businesses and one that makes for professional attitudes that fit in with the economic targets of business and other organizations. There is only one prior requirement: continued education and training of everyone involved in tourism from consumers to those responsible for tourist policies. The demand for quality, and even more so, for environmental quality, is a call to people's awareness, to their understanding of the environmental and cultural implications of any activity and their ability to express themselves and to organize to choose the most clear-sighted line of action.

Growth of Tourism in India

Tourism is a high growth industry globally. Though currently only 3.5 per cent of the world's population travels internationally, by 2020, this figure is expected to double. In India as well, economic growth and infrastructure development are expected to increase tourist arrivals: the World tourism Organisation projects a 7.5 per cent annual increase in the number of tourist arrivals in India till 2001.

The tourism sector which has witnessed a growth of 500 per cent over the past decade has registered a growth of 14.4 per cent for the period of January to April in 2006 as compared to the corresponding period, the year before. While, on one hand the number of outbound tourists increased by a whopping 16.1 per cent last year, the international holiday maker's penchant for India grew by 11.4 per cent. No wonder we stand fourth in the list of 'most attractive destinations in the world', according to Conde Nast Reader's Travel awards, 2006.

Also worth appreciation is the way brand 'India' has been marketed to the outside world... especially with the 'Incredible India' campaign that cost the government a monstrous Rs.60 crore, but has done more than its fair share to prop up Indian tourism worldwide.

A noticeable change in the holidaying trend has been reported, where both – the international and domestic tourists showed inclination towards adventure sports which can be reinforced with the fact that the industry witnesses two million adventure aficionados every year. With 7,600 Kilometre of a magnificent coastline, the grandiose Himalayas, 12 major rivers and a myriad variety of wildlife. What else remains to be said?

The majestic Himalayas stretching across its boarders, lush green forests, the warm breeze kissed by the vast ocean, the silvery, sun-kissed beaches and the spiritual havens-this is not all that we have to offer! Incredible India transcends all definitions of scenic magnificence and grandeur and surpasses all comparisons. What was only known as the land of elephants and snake charmers in yesteryears, now boasts of world-class infrastructure, swanky cities, IT parks, shopping malls and booming economy, amalgamated with the country's innocent back-waters of Kerala, the naughty beaches of Goa, the pristine peaks of Kashmir and the still untouched North-eastern territories!

Indian tourism industry has recorded a phenomenal growth especially from 1990's in terms of both international and domestic tourist's arrivals. According to Table 23.1 18,86,433 foreigners visited as tourists in India, accounting for 0.34 per cent of the tourists in the world. In the succeeding year the foreign tourist arrivals in India went up to 21,23,683, accounting for 0.38 per cent of the world tourists. This trend continued up to 2000, as can be seen in the table.

Table 23.1: International Tourist Arrivals to India

Year	Tourist arrivals (India)	Tourist arrivals (world, in Million)	Percentage share of India
1994	18,86,433	550.3	0.34
1995	21,23,683	565.4	0.38
1996	22,87,860	597.4	0.38
1997	23,74,094	618.2	0.38
1998	23,58,629	626.7	0.38
1999	24,81,928	650.0	0.38
2000	26,41,157	698.3	0.38

Source: India Tourist Statistics, 1999, issued by Market Research Division, Department of Tourism, Govt. of India.

With regard to the growth of domestic tourists in India it is maintained that 6.38 crore people visited different tourist places in the country. One can absorb Table 23.2 that there has been a steady growth in the domestic tourists in India and by 1999 the total

Domestic tourists arrivals recorded was 17.60 crore which is not a mean progress in this regard. The inference that one can drop from this table is that there is a sustained growth in the tourism in India.

Table 23.2: Domestic Tourist Arrivals to India

Year	Domestic Tourist Arrivals
1990	6,38,17,285
1991	8,58,64,892
1992	10,24,65,705
1993	10,92,37,566
1994	12,71,16,655
1995	13,66,48,600
1996	14,01,19,672
1997	15,98,71,008
1998	16,81,96,000
1999	17,60,82,442

Source: Market Research Division, Department of Tourism, Govt. of India.

Growth of Tourism in Andhra Pradesh

As mentioned earlier that tourism even at the state level of Andhra Pradesh shows an encouraging trend, especially, after 1990's. The total number of domestic tourist arrivals in Andhra Pradesh for the year 1993 was recorded at 2.67 crore; slowly it picked up its momentum and by the year 2002 the total domestic tourist arrivals in Andhra Pradesh stood at 6.33 crore.

The encouraging trend is being observed even in the case of international tourists in Andhra Pradesh. The total number of international tourists for the year 1993 was 47,200 which went up to 94,400 by 1997 and by 2002 the international tourists arrivals in Andhra Pradesh was 2,10,310 implying the fact that international tourists over a period of 10 years, 1993-2002 was nearly 4.5 times, vide Table 23.3.

Growth of Tourism in Chittoor District

Chittoor district is one of the important tourist destinations in the country in view of the world famous temple towns: Tirupati, Srikalahasti and Kanipakam; Hill Resort of Madanapalli Horsley Hills and beautiful waterfalls at Talakona. These tourist places in the district attract the largest domestic tourists in the entire country and a considerable foreign pilgrims too. To provide impetus to the tourism sector in the district all out efforts have been made to extend modern infrastructure in terms of Lodges, boarding houses, all-weather roads, railways, airways along with Star Hotels in Tirupati. An attempt is made here to study the Sustainable Tourism development in Chittoor District.

Table 23.3: Tourist Arrivals in Andhra Pradesh and Expenditure Patterns

S. No.	Year	Domestic Tourists (crore)	International Tourist arrivals
1.	1993	2.67	47,200
2.	1994	3.28	48,700
3.	1995	3.93	84,100
4.	1996	3.35	63,600
5.	1997	3.68	94,400
6.	1998	3.84	78,976
7.	1999	4.23	86,310
8.	2000	4.80	78,713
9.	2001	5.25	1,54,623
10.	2002	6.33	2,10,310

Source: Andhra Pradesh Tourism Department, Hyderabad.

The domestic tourists' arrivals in a decade, from 1995 to 2004 in all the five tourist places of Chittoor District have been displayed in Table 23.4. The total number of domestic tourists' arrivals in all the five places put together for the year 1995 was 1,49,58,564 this has short up 3,16,01,641 for the year 2004. That means the tourist arrivals in all the five places increased year after year and in a span of ten years the tourist arrivals was more than doubled in the district.

With regard to foreign tourist arrivals for the above 5 places for the same period have been displayed in Table 23.5. The total number of foreign tourist arrivals was 500 for the year 1995 and it

Table 23.4: Particulars of Tourists' Arrivals and Proceeds in Chittoor District for a Decade from 1995-2004

Year	Tirupati – Tirumala		Srikalahasti		Kanipakam		Horsley Hills	
	Domestic Tourist arrivals	Tourists Income (Rs. crore)	Domestic Tourist arrivals	Tourists Income (Rs. in crore)	Domestic Tourist arrivals	Tourists Income (Rs. in crore)	Domestic Tourist arrivals	Tourists Income (Rs. lakh)
1995	1,27,47,654	512	7,34,900	3.99	14,20,430	2.26	3,200	16.05
1996	1,43,93,463	529	9,49,860	4.90	16,05,970	2.49	4,986	17.19
1997	1,52,84,963	538	11,40,940	5.10	17,60,860	3.05	6,091	18.70
1998	1,64,32,600	550	13,24,620	5.98	19,86,920	3.60	7,640	20.49
1999	1,72,41,860	562	18,40,020	6.99	21,09,710	3.92	8,209	22.30
2000	1,81,50,433	576	23,51,000	7.97	22,45,990	4.32	9,181	25.47
2001	1,92,40,955	589	28,66,300	9.20	23,50,340	4.90	9,875	28.92
2002	21462811	602	39,25,400	11.39	24,09,910	5.20	11,040	34.83
2003	2,21,39,255	615	46,76,900	12.64	25,90,860	6.01	11,810	44.74
2004	2,32,76,890	633	54,68,900	13.51	27,18,600	6.82	12,311	64.42

Source: Tourism Department Office, Tirupati.

Table 23.5: Foreign Tourist Arrivals in Chittoor District

Year	Tirupati	Srikalahasti	Kanipakam	Talakona	Horsley Hills	Total Foreign Tourist Arrivals
1995	397	86	10	3	4	500
1996	410	69	18	5	3	505
1997	427	80	23	4	4	538
1998	390	89	31	7	6	516
1999	370	94	43	6	5	496
2000	401	90	43	9	3	526
2001	413	93	46	10	6	548
2002	398	91	44	12	5	533
2003	369	90	47	11	4	499
2004	418	93	46	12	7	556
Grand Total						5217

Source: Tourism Department Office, Tirupati.

increased to 556 for the year 2004. The table reveals that there was a steady flow of foreign tourist arrivals in Chittoor District. The total number of foreign tourist arrivals over a period of decade was just 5217.

Proceeds from Tourism

The total proceeds of the tourist arrivals- both the domestic and the foreign tourist arrivals at Tirupati was Rs.512 crore for the year 1995 and it short up to Rs. 633 crore by 2004.

In the case of Srikalahasti the tourist proceeds for the year 1995 was Rs. 3.99 crore and it increased Rs. 31.51 crore by 2004.

An amount of Rs.2.26 crore obtained as tourists' proceeds at Kanipakam. The total proceeds of tourists' arrivals was Rs.6.82 crore by 2004.

In the case of Horsley Hills at Madanapalli and Talakona the total proceeds for the year 1995 was respectively Rs. 16.05 lakh and Rs. 2.46 lakh. The tourists' arrivals proceeds at Horsley Hills Madanapalli and Talakona for the year 2004 was respectively Rs. 64.42 lakh and Rs. 3.74 lakh.

Conclusion

According to a conservative estimate more than 15,000 persons are directly employed on a permanent basis in all the five tourist places in the district. It is not an exaggerating thing that more than two lakh people eke out sustenance from these five tourists places through rendering various services- transport and communication, board and lodging, grocers shops, handy crafts, flower vending, sale of decorative goods, and travel agencies.

It is learnt through primary survey that there is a great tourist potential remained unexplored in all the places. Talakona and Madanapalli Horsley Hills badly suffer for want of modern infrastructure facilities; if they are equipped with the necessary modern infrastructure and the same is made known to the public at large through appropriate media, certainly these two places along with the remaining three tourist places in the district will attract a good number of both domestic and foreign tourists and thus pushup the economy of the district through the tourist proceeds. The Andhra Pradesh Tourism may concentrate its attention to draw up suitable plans and implement them for the development of the tourist places in Chittoor District as tourism richly rewards the district with good returns.

References

Anand, Sanjay (1997), "New tourism policy will focus on higher earnings", in The Times of India, New Delhi, March: 18.

Babu, A.Satish (1999), "Tourism Development in India", A.P.H. Publishing Corporation, New Delhi, pp. 20-48.

Chopra, S. (1991), "Tourism and Development in India", Ashish Publishing House, New Delhi.

Fennell, D. (1999), "Ecotourism-An Introduction", Routledge, London, HRAI Magazine and Newsletter 2000, Vol.2; March: 12.

Helen Braissoulis and Jan Vander Straiten: Tourism and the Environment Regional, Economic, Cultural and Policy and issues, Kluwer Academic Publishers, London, 2000.

Holloway, J.C. (1994): The Business of Tourism, Pitman, London.

Inskeep E. "Tourism Planning: An Integrated and Sustainable Development Approach", Van Nostrand Reinhold, New York.

Mathew, P.M. (2003), "Natural Environment and Tourist Inflow", Environmental changes towards Tourism, Kanishka Publishers, New Delhi.

Nagi, J. "Tourism Development and Resources and conservation", Metropolitan, New Delhi.

Przeclawski, K. (1993), "Tourism as the subject of inter-disciplinary research", in Rstaurant and Administration Quarterly, Vol.11 (2), pp.9-19.

Ranga, Mukesh (2003), "Tourism Potential in India", Abhijeet Publications, New Delhi, pp. 45-48.

Romila Chawla (2003), "Tourism Research Planning and Development", Sonali Publications, 4831/24, Ansari Road, Prahlad Street, Darya Ganj, New Delhi.

Stabler MJ(ed) (1997), "Tourism Sustainability: Principles and Practices", CAB, International, Oxon.

World Tourism Organisation (2001), WTO News.

24

Tourism Potential in Backward Areas of Andhra Pradesh

Tourism emerged as the fastest growing industry in the world. Tourism Industry in India too has gained its momentum and it is able to generate a considerable direct and indirect employment and earn foreign exchange to the economy to a greater extent. In addition to this tourism has a multi-fact advantage to the economy. Given the dimensions and tourist potentials which exist in Andhra Pradesh, there is a tremendous scope and urgency to declare tourism as an industry and extend all possible direct and indirect support for its accelerated growth in the State. Realizing this fact, the Government of Andhra Pradesh declared "tourism as an industry" and resolved to extend several benefits and concessions to the individuals and organizations that are actively indeed in the affairs of tourism industry. Tourism is undoubtedly the largest business in the world. The recent urge in business and pleasure travel represents an unparalleled demand for tourism related services. This demand has been filled by a growing world economy. The continued increase in world wide tourism has encouraged both private investors and Governments and it rapidly expand the facilities to better serve tourists and business travelers. Which has raised the standard of living of millions of people around the globe?

Tourism potential impact on economy, environment and people are now fully recognised. It is multi-faced. It is an industry creating jobs, earning foreign currency and generating tax revenues. Tourism also stands out as an ever present factor in promoting mutual knowledge and understanding and therefore peace and detento. India, because of its rich cultural traditions, historical background and variated geographical conditions has become one of the major tourist attractions in this part of the globe, its colorful geographical features, historical and cultural mosaic and its fauna and flora and beaches offer not only a pleasant climate of all times of the year, in some part or the other, of our vast country, but a sense of sharing a heritage.

A fine bend of tradition and modernity which is available in plenty in India enhances the appeal of this country as a "Tourism country". Tourism was declared as an industry in 1988. In India it enjoys bright prospects and is estimated that in 1995 tourism gave employment to six million people, besides yielding a million to the exchequer. The Department of Tourism and Indian Tourism Development Corporation in close association with approves Hotels and Travel Agencies extend facilities that are related to the tourism promotion in the country". It was only in the VII Plan period that tourism was recognized as an important activity.

India has several attracting resorts for tourists, most of them are situated in Delhi, Mumbai, Agra, Chennai, Kolkata, Varanasi, Amritsar, Jaipur, Srinagar, Bangalore, Khajuraho, Tiruchinapalli, Patna, Goa, Mysore, Aurangabad, Kochi, Madurai, Tirupati and Udaipur. However total numbers of such places are virtually more than hundred in the country. Delhi, the capital city, is the top-most attraction for foreign tourists arriving in India.

Discover Andhra Pradesh: A Tourist Paradise

One can discover a confluence of the North and South Indian cultures in Andhra Pradesh as one descends from the lofty Himalayas to Kanyakumari. Andhra Pradesh offers a homogenous blending of ancient and modern, northern and southern multi-lingual and multi-racial cultures. The rich literacy heritage of Telugu, the principal language of the State, and the second largest language spoken in the country prides itself of the triumvirate Nannaya, Tikkana and Errapragada, the Ashtadiggajas of Sri Krishnadevaraya in the medieval period and Jnanapeeth award recipients Shri Viswanadha Satyanarayana and Dr. C. Narayana Reddy in the contemporary period.

Andhra Pradesh is popularly known as the granary of India. The lush green fields, naturally irrigated by 34 rivers including the major ones, Krishna and Godavari, provide the scenic beauty while the centres of heritage entice the tourists to visit the State again and again. A single example is Tirupati, the abode of Sri Venkateswara, where pilgrims from all parts of the country throng for a glimpse of the Lord. For the tourist, the State provides all kinds of attractions like water falls, lakes, forests, hill and coastline, while the hospitable and cosmopolitan Andhra Pradesh make him feel at home.

The capital city, Hyderabad itself has a history of over 400 years. Founded by Quali Qutub Shah in 1591, the city offers a variety of attractions like the Charminar and its nearby Mocca Masjid, the Salarjung Museum, one of the largest one-man collection of antiques in the world and the impregnable Golconda fort with its excellent acoustics.

Warangal is equally famous as the seat of Kakatiya empire during the 11th-13th centuries. The exquisitely carved Ramappa temple near Warangal is famous as the "Brightest star of the galaxy of medieval temples of the Deccan". Enroute to Warangal from Hyderabad is the 2000 year old Jain Mahavira temple at Kolanupaka where a museum is also located. Srisailam around 230 kms. from Hyderabad, stand the ancient as well as modern temples. Both Ramappa and Srisailam are located in thick forests and are famous for wild life sanctuaries in which tiger, leopard, bear and other wild animals can be seen in their natural habitat. Vijayawada, the central place in Andhra Pradesh, both literally and culturally, is another famous tourist attraction.

Kondapalli, noted for toy-making is just at a stone's throw from Vijayawada. Around 70 kms. from Vijayawada is Managinapudi where the golden beach provides immense relief. It is a safe beach because the shallow waters offer not only enjoyment but also pleasant scenery. The frescos of Lepakshi temple are no less in grandeur to the cave paintings of Ajanta and Ellora. Puttaparti, about 50 kms. from Lepakshi is a modern pilgrimage, Centre for the spiritual minded tourist. The importance of tourism in Andhra Pradesh was recognised very late and tourism was a part of the Information and Public

Relations Department till May, 1974 when it was separated and established as Department of Tourism. In 1980, the State Travel and Tourism Development Corporation were unveiled. Tourism became an officially recognised industry in 1985 and certain types of hotels where extended concessions and subsidies.

In 1990, a 17 Member Tourism Board was established to advise the Government about the development of tourism in the State. In 1994, the Government of Andhra Pradesh announced its Tourism Policy declaring certain places as special tourist centres. The present paper is aimed at discussing the tourist potential in Chittoor district. Tourist potentials or attractions are those elements which determine the choice of the tourist and also development of tourism. The other factors like accommodation, transportation, catering, entertainment etc., could be referred to as tourism context factors which serve as the secondary ones. Hence, this paper exclusively covers the tourism potentials in the district.

The very mention of Chittoor district reminds one of the famous temples which have historic importance. Besides being a premier religious district, Chittoor also has a number of tourist spots to its credit and every year lakh of pilgrims and tourists visit the district.

Geographical Background of the District

Chittoor district is one of the 23 districts of Andhra Pradesh and southern most part of four districts of Rayalaseema as well as Andhra Pradesh. The district derived its name from Chittoor, its head quarter's town. It is located between the northern latitudes of 12° 37′ and 14° 8′ and the eastern longitudes of 78° 31′ and 79° 55′. It is bounded on the east by Nellore district of Andhra Pradesh and Changalepat district of Tamil Nadu, on the west by Kolar district of Karnataka, on the north to a great extent by Kadapa and Anantapur districts of Andhra Pradesh and on the south by North Arcot and Dharmapuri districts of Tamil Nadu. In respect of the area it takes the 8th place with an area of 15,188.56 Square Kms. which accounts for 5.51 per cent of the total area of the State.

The district may regularly be divided into two regions, namely (i) the hills and up lands and (ii) the plains. The plains, valleys plateau and the hills combine to make this district, one of the most picturesque in the State. The imposing Seshachalam hills, over which the famous pilgrim centre of Tirupati is located, is perhaps one of the most picturesque spots in this part of the country.

Tourism Potential

On the whole tourism sector has immense potentiality in improving the socio-economic status of rural population and not to say of urban population. Further, thrust on this sector will naturally give an impetus to the speedy overall development of the district. This district has virtually got potentiality to develop all kinds of tourism such as, heritage, religious, nature, leisure, eco tourism etc. ***"Chittoor district is the pilgrimage heart – Tirumala-Tirupati – Vatican of India."*** The Eastern Ghats form a major range of hills in Andhra Pradesh starting in the southern-most district of Chittoor. Chittoor district lies the temple town of Tirumala with Tirupati at the foot hills. The range of hills is said to resemble a snake with Tirumal forming the bond, Lord Venkateswara. Hence as Lord of the Seven hills and Balaji, is the 'Kaliyuga' incarnation of Lord Vishnu. Tirupati and Tirumala today have destinations of pilgrim tourists. Not only the bliss of a divine 'darshan' but added attractions provided by nature make them the ideal pilgrimage-cum-holiday destination.

Places of Tourist Interest in and Around Tirupati and Tirumala Lord Venkateswara Temple

The temple of Balaji at Tirumala hills is famous in the world and more than millions of pilgrims from across the globe visit the temple annually.

Swami Puskarini: Many of the pilgrims have dip in the tank adjacent to the temple at Tirumala, before having a Darshan of Lord Venkateswara.

Akasa Ganga: Significant future here is that Ganga always flows from the feet of idol About 3 Kms. north of the main temple is a perennial stream that is said to flow from the feet of the deity. The most l.

Sila Thoranam: Sila Thoranam is a rare geological formation, believed to be several million years old, situated 1 Km north of the Venkateswara Temple. It is natural rock formation in the form of an arch, near Chakra Teertham and is a must-see place, every day visit the pilgrims.

Kapila Teertham: Lord Shiva is said to have appeared before sage Kapila in the historic place. The cascading waterfalls from the holy hills are a treat to watch.

Sri Prasanna Venkateswara Swamy Temple: Sri Prasanna Venkateswara Swamy temple is an ancient temple located at Appalayakunta which is 15 Kms. from Tirupati.

Sri Venugopala Swamy Temple: Sri Venugopala Swamy temple is situated in Karvetinagar, which is 58 Kms. from Tirupati.

Sri Govindaraja Swamy Temple: It is the biggest temple in Tirupati. Interestingly, this is the only idol in the country for which no abhishekam is performed as it is made of clay.

Alamelu Mangapuram: No visit to Tirupati is complete without a visit to Alamelu Mangapuram. Lord Viswakarma is said to have built the magnificent temple for Goddess Padmavathi.

Sreenivasa Mangapuram: Lying 12 Kms. to the west of Tirupati, Sreenivasa Managapuram is a small village where Lord Venkateswara and Goddess Padmavathi are believed to have stayed for sometime after their marriage.

Narayanvanam: This is where the marriage between Lord Venkateswara and Goddess Padmavathi is said to have taken place. Located 38 Kms. from Tirupati.

Sri Venkateswara Zoological Park: Spread over an area of 2.5 acres and located near Alipiri Gate. This unique park has been conceived and developed by the Regional Science Centre, a unit of the National Council of Science Museums. Entry fee is Rs. 5

per head, and Rs. 2 per head for organized school groups. Open on all days from 10 AM to 6 PM.

Chandragiri: The Fort atop a huge rock that stands 56 meters tall is just 12 Kms. from the temple town of Tirupati. AP Tourism has put together a unique Sound & Light Show at Chandragiri to relive the glory of the Vijayanagar Empire. After a hectic trip to temples and shrines in and around Tirupati, it is time for the much-needed relaxation at Chandragiri, a perfect way to round off the day.

On the National Highway to Chennai, about 50 Kms. from Tirupati, a way-side amenity has been created by the APTDC on 4.5 across of land just out of Puttur town.

Facilities

AP Tourism offers excellent accommodation at Puttur Highway Resort, on the highway from Tirupati to Chennai. This resort comes with specious parking, accommodation and 50-seater restaurant and bar.

Table 24.1 gives the information regarding the Revenue from accommodation and catering from 1998 to 2003. In the year 1998-99 Revenue from accommodation and catering was Rs.142 lakh. It was increased every year and in the year 2002-2003 revenue from accommodation and catering was Rs. 700.04 lakh.

Table: 24.1 Revenue from Accommodation and Catering

Year	Amount (Rs. lakh)
1998-1999	142.00
1999-2000	229.84
2000-2001	290.65
2001-2002	400.08
2002-2003	700.04

Source: APTDC Office, Tirupati

Tourism Attractions

One of the latest and most modern properties that have come

up recently is the highway resort at Kuppam in Chittoor district. Like all such amenities, it is christened **"Punnami"** built at a cost of Rs. 300 lakh.

Facilities

There are 12 A/C rooms, 8 Non-A/C rooms and 24 bed dormitory, a restaurant and bar, Swimming pool, 300 seater amphi theatre, a 50 seater conference hall, children's play area, Fitness centre, petrol filling station, Souvenir shop, information centre and adequate parking area. Room service is other amenities added. Regarding the accommodation facilities in Punnami highway resort, Kuppam. Rates are ranging from Rs. 75 to 500.

Table 24.2 gives clear information regarding the category-wise tourism potential in Chittoor district. There are different categories of tourism places in this district like pilgrim centers, heritage centers, holiday resorts, national parks, historic places and some religion and Picnic spots which includes some world famous pilgrim places. Besides these two tourists high way resorts are also present.

Table: 24.2 Category-wise Tourism Potential in Chittoor District

Sl. No.	Place	Category
1	Tirupati-Tirumala	Pilgrim centre
2	Sree Kalaasti	Pilgrim centre
3	Kanipakam	Pilgrim centre
4	Narayana vanam	Pilgrim centre
5	Chandragiri	Historical place
6	Gudimallam	Heritage centre
7	Madanapalle	Holiday resort
8	Rishi valley	Holiday resort
9	Horsley hills	Holiday resort
10	Talakona	Holiday resort
11	Kailasanatha Kona	Holiday resort

Contd...

12	Sri Venkateswara Wild life Sancturary	National Park
13	Sreenivasa Mangapuram	Historical place
14	Urban Haat	World famous pilgrim town
15	Kalyani dam	Picnic place
16	Gurram Konda	Historical place
17	Reddemma Konda	Pilgrim centre
18	Sompalyam	Historical place
19	Boya Konda	Pilgrim place
20	Karvetinagar	Temple place
21	Nagalapuram	Historical place
22	Mogili	Tourist place
23	Kalyana revulu	Waterfalls
24	Ganganna Sirrassu	Waterfalls
25	Koundinya Elephant Sancturary	Zoo park
26	Dumukurallu waterfalls	Picnic place
27	Kangudi	Historical place
28	Gudivanka	Religious and picnic spot
29	Kuppam	Tourist High way resort
30	Puttur	Tourist High way resort

Source: Department of Tourism, Tirupati.

Accommodation Facilities

In the district there are several types of hotels are covered all the tourist places. Table 24.3 gives the information regarding the strength of hotel accommodation in Chittoor district.

Chittoor district has a very high potential in accommodation facilities. There are 6 Punnami Resort hotels, 12 Star hotels (III Star and II Star), 8 Janatha hotels, 7 Choultries, in overage all tourist places in the entire district. Tirupati-Tirumala temple town is having 8 star hotels and 12 Janatha hotels and 85 general hotels.

Tourism facilities in the district are: 1. Accommodation 2. Travel agencies, 3. Catering service; 4. Bar service; 5. Package tours; 6. Fair and Festivals; 7. Sight-seeing facilities; 8.Public relations; 9. Adventure sports; 10. Boating facilities; 11. Entertainment complexes; 12.Health farms; 13.Amusement parks; 14.Heritage hotels; 15.Motels/Way side; 16. Resorts.

Table: 24.3 Strength of Hotel Accommodation

Hotel	Place	Rooms
High way resort	Kuppam	21
High way resort	Puttur	6
Hill resort	Horsley hills	39
Jungle resort	Talakona	12
Valley resort	Kailasanatha Kona	8
Sreenivasam complex	Tirupati	140
Sreenivasam	Tirumala	8
Star hotels (12)	Tirupati	873
Choultries (7)	Tirumala	1215
Janatha hotels (8)	Tirumala	395

Source: Tourism Department, Tirupati.

Andhra Pradesh Tourism Development Corporation Limited is the implementation wing of development of tourism. Chittoor district is extremely rich and has varied tourism resources. It offers historical monuments, pilgrim sites, wild life, archaeological relics and hill stations. Handicrafts, art, music and folk dances offer additional reasons for the tourist to visit Chittoor district.

Tirupati-Tirumala attracts lakh of tourists every year. 40 Travel agencies, 30 tourist guides, 50 tourist drivers, and the hotel industry has greatly benefited out of ever in increasing tourist traffic. Chittoor district has accorded tourism, the status of an industry and is placing emphasis on the creation of tourism infrastructure. The benefits are shared by a large number of segments/groups viz. hotels and restaurants, travel agents and tour operators, passenger transport services, entertainment establishments, sales outlets, culture and guide services. Ethnic tourism has gained considerable popularity. This form of rural tourism encourages local communities to preserve their ethnic culture and gives employment opportunities at the local level. Tirupati has many places of religious significance in rural areas. Such destinations are an attraction for the domestic tourists.

In Tirupati region there are several centres which are famous for terra cotta, wooden toys, Jewellery boxes, paintings and jewellery etc. An important initiative has come from the Government in the arts and crafts village at Tirupati. This centre provides an opportunity to rural artists to interact through camps and workshops. It is estimated that by the year 2005, actively will generate additional employment for 3.59 million persons in the State. The estimated employment of women is taken as 20 per cent of total employment.

References

Bhargava, S.C., "Socio-Economic Benefits of Tourism Development in India, Monthly Commentary," Vol. XXXII, No. 18, 383, June, 1991.

Hugh and Colleen Gantzer, "Tourism 2000: The great white hope," The Hindu Magazine, Sunday, Jan. 8, 1995.

John, M. Bryden, Tourism and Development – A Case Study of the Commonwealth Caribbean Overseas Development Group, University of East Anglia, p. 23.

Navin Chandra Joshi, Tourism Industry needs boosting, *Yojana*, October, 16, 1990.

Satya Sundaram, I., Tourism, a multi-dimensional Industry, Facts for You, April, 1991.

Sivasankara Bhat, K., Promoting Indian Tourism, *Southern Economist*, Vol. 29, No. 1, May 1, 1990.

Vidya Sagar Reddy, G., "Tourism Industry in Andhra Pradesh," Sri Krishnadevaraya University, Anantapur, Ph.D. Thesis, 1996, p. 1.

25

Socio-economic Impact of Tourism in Developing Countries

Introduction

Tourism has been especially important in the developing world, which stands to suffer severe economic losses from the slow down. "Tourism is the only economic sector where developing countries consistently run a trade surplus," says Mastany. "It's especially significant in poorer countries that have few other options: for the world's 49 so-called least developed countries, tourism is the second largest source of foreign exchange after oil." The word "Tourist" became current early in the 19th century as a same what contemptuous synonym for traveler, but it is now used in the social sciences without colour, to describes any person whose movements fulfill two conditions that first, absence from home is relatively short and second, that money spent during absence is money derived from home and not earned in the places visited.

Thus tourists may be sightseers, any travelers who, as distinct, from immigrants or emigrants, intend to return home within, say, twelve months and who, as a distinct from migratory labourers, move in the capacity of consumers, not producers. From the very earliest period, travel has always a fascination for man. There are numerous accounts of some foreign traveler who visited India notably among them was Alexander the Great, Vasco-da-Gama, Columbus, Marco Polo, Francisco-Fair and John of Monte Corrine, besides, many more European monks and adventures. India, reasons for their travel had been different, they may be for conquering, pleasure, knowledge or trade, the conclusion in that India like many other countries of the world has been famous among the tourist community.

The travel and tourism buzzword of the 21st century will be the search for balance. The identification, maintenance and management of this entrance of balance will be the single most important requirement for the tourism industry of the 21st century. Those companies, institutions and destinations that perform the balancing act well will attain the elusive goal of sustainable development. Tourism is a business of providing and entertainment for tourists. Tourism as we understand the term today is of relatively modern origin. It is a business, which creates to the need of the tourists like providing lodging, transport, entertainment and information. Tourism is the developing world, is particularly worried about the sharp drop in bookings as the winter high season nears.

- India and Nepal, which are close to Afghanistan, are already feeling the effects of a drop in demand.
- In October, resort company club Mediterranean was forced to close 15 of its holiday villages in the Caribbean, Central America, the Middle East, Europe, and Asia.
- Operators in Costa Rica resort a 30 per cent decline in bookings from last year.
- International Tourism is now expected to grow by only 1.5 to 2 per cent in 2001, compared with the robust 7.4 per cent rise in the year 2000.
- The International Labour Organization estimates that as many of 9 million of the world's 200 million hotel and tourism workers could lose their jobs in the wake of the attacks. Nearly three quarters of these positions are outside the United States and Europe, many in countries with weak social safety nets.

Factors Responsible for Growth of Tourism

Tourism is developed rapidly only after the end of the world war. The basic causes of steady growth of tourism are economic, social and technological in nature.

Raising per capita income, leading to higher purchasing power and an increase in discretionary incomes have made tourism accessible to a large majority of people.

To-day in advanced countries, a large majority of people can afford holidays of longer of shorter duration. In the case of more affluent members of the society, establishment of recreation homes, like seaside flats, counter cottages, caravans, crushing boats, have become a fashion and status symbol. Secondly more and diverse types of holiday recreations are becoming such as yachting, riding, safari, skiing, mountaineering, boating and sports. The spectacular improvements in the means of transport, communication and infrastructural facilities are the more important economic factors responsible for growth in tourism.

The social causes for the rapid growth of tourism are linked with new attitudes towards travel leisure. Foreign travel in the pre-war days reserved for more affluent and leisured who enjoyed travel for its own shake.

The concept has now changed with the change in attitudes towards travel. The present day tourist has a different kind of background, and his ideas about travel are very different.

He comes from a wider social background and his tastes and ambitions are much more varied. His leisure time is limited and accordingly he thinks of packing into it as much as possible. Sports that are confirmed to rich society people do not attract the ordinary tourist who can well afford to participate in other sports such as riding, boating, yachting, shooting, mountaineering, tracking, under water swimming and the like in countries where these are made available.

The impact of the modern technology, especially in aviation field has brought about a completely new meaning to tourism. Travel to long distant destinations has now become a reality. The technological developments in transport have made it possible for millions of people to travel to far away places.

The marketing methods like the package tour and holiday trips complete with all arrangements like transport, accommodation, sightseeing and selling these on a large scale to intending public have brought down significantly by the average cost per tour which is much below the cost of the trip arranged individually. Opening of new travel destinations particularly in developing countries, creation of new facilities to receive bigger inflow of tourists and increasing tourism promoting efforts by tourist service enterprises have further pushed up the tourist inflows. In the hopes of raping the benefits that could result from actively soliciting travelers, many Governments have been engaged in large and colourful advertising campaign in magazines, newspapers and ultimately in Televisions.

Economic and Social Significance of Tourism

During the 1960's tourism was considered as a source of foreign exchange, a catalyst of development and security against the uncertain fluctuations in the economy.

To-day, tourism's status as a major economic activity is recognized through the world. On the recommendation of the National Development Council (NDC) various State Government declared tourism as an industry.

Economic Significance: The receipt from international tourism provides a valuable source of earnings from many countries both developed as well as developing. Tourism provides more sizeable earnings than primary products. The income from tourism tends to increase at a higher rate than merchandise export and it is an assured changed of financial flows from developed countries to developing countries, raising the latter's export earnings and rate of economic growth.

The income from foreign tourism in the form of foreign exchange adds to the national income and as invisible export, reduces the loss in the overall financial position. The invisible which come from transport and shipping, banking and insurance, income on investments, etc., utilized by tourists visiting the host country, influence the balance of payments of the country.

The foreign exchange earnings from tourism which were estimated at Rs. 1,063 crore in 1981 increased to Rs. 1,189 crore in 1985, Rs. 1,856 crore in 1987 Rs. 2,456 crore in 1990. Rs. 3,249 crore in 1995. Rs. 4,105 crore in 2000. Rs. 5,238 crore in 2004.

Tourist facilities such as hotel, public transport, museums, clubs, and sports complexes. National parks are also used by domestic tourists and visitors although a significant portion of the costs is borne by foreign tourists. Tourists also contribute to tax revenue both directly through sales tax and indirectly through property profits and income taxes. Tourism provides employment. Tourist expenditure not only supports the tourist industry but also helps indirectly to support many other industries, which supply goods and services to the tourist industry. Thus the money spent by the tourists after a series of transfers over a period passes through all sectors of the economy, stimulating each in turn throughout the in economic terms is called multiplier effect.

Development and improvement of infrastructure is another important benefit. The benefits from infrastructure investments on airports, roads, water supply and other public utilities, primarily made available for foreign tourists are widely by other sectors of the economy.

Another important economic effect of tourism is related to regional development of isolated and economically under developed areas. Many of such regions having high scenic beauty and cultural attractions can become areas of great interest for tourists bringing property to the local people. Khajuraho which is now an internationally famous spot was a remote and unknown small village about 20 years ago. The development of Khajuraho as a world famous tourist resort has resulted in the acceleration of many economic and social activities, providing employment and prosperity to a large population of the area. Similarly, with a view to bring development and prosperity, a number of under developed regions have been developed for attracting tourists.

Another major direct economic effect of tourism is related to employment. Most of the developing countries are facing problems of unemployment and under-employment. The tourist industry is a valuable source of employment to a large number of people from the unskilled to waiters, cooks, managers, executives in hotels, transport, constructing hotels, roads, airports, water supply and other public utilities, the basic infrastructures for tourism promotion creates jobs for thousands of skilled and unskilled workers.

Social Significance: Besides economic benefits to a country by way of earning foreign exchange, employment generation, regional development and bringing prosperity to the people as the primary objectives, tourism also makes a massive contribution to the social and political understanding. Tourism is thus an important means of promoting cultural exchanges and international co-operation. At the same time, it must be recognized that tourism also contributed to the protection of the natural environment and cultural heritage of people and in particular to the restoration of historic and archaeological buildings and works of art. Nature parks in many parts of the world have been established in the interest of tourism, that protecting landscape, fauna and flora from destruction by modern development. The survival of traditional handicrafts has been promoted as a tourist attraction and thus contributed to the preservation of the national heritage. Historic buildings have been restored and revitalized as tourism facilities. Archaeological sites have been excavated to attract tourism and many other examples of tourism, as promoter and protector of our National Human Environment come to mind

Promotion of Basic Components of Tourism: Any place for promoting tourism, should have at least any one of the basic components. They are

- Scenic view
- Historical and cultural attractions
- Religious significance
- Bird and Wildlife sanctuaries, and
- Philanthropic significance.

Scenic View: Scenery or landscape consisting of beautiful hill stations, lakes, water falls, glaciers, beaches, forests etc., are strong force tempting tourists to visit them. The Himalayan mountain slopes, that lakes of Kashmir and Udaipur, glaciers of Himachal and Upper Ladakh, beautiful beaches of Goa, forest of Assam, Bengal, Karnataka and Deserts of Rajasthan are charmed by physical magnificence and are a great source of attraction to many tourists.

Historical and Cultural Attractions: Places having historical and cultural attractions have propounded influence on the tourist. Large number of tourists are attracted every year by Taj Mahal, Red Fort, Qutubminar, Caves of Ajantha and Ellora and many other historical monuments. Similarly cultural attractions like Dussehra festival of Kulu, Vishnapur festival of West Bengal and Camel Safari festival of Rajasthan are some of the cultural festivals that attract most of the foreign tourists. There are many areas which, because of history and cultural attractions can be potential tourist resorts.

Religious Significance: Places having religious significance also attract a large number of tourists. Religious places like Varanasi, Kedaranath, in the north and Tirupati, Srikalahasti, Kanipakam and Sabarimalai in the south and various other places in India have attracted large number of tourists. Thus there is a scope for development of tourism in the places having religious importance.

Bird and Wildlife Sanctuaries: Bird and wildlife sanctuaries also have propound influence on the tourists. Bird and wildlife sanctuaries like Tekadi in Kerala, Badhipur and Ranganathittu in Karnataka Sri Venkateswara wildlife sanctuary, Tirupati in A.P. have gained tourists importance. Places having these sanctuaries can be developed into tourist centres.

Philanthropic: There are many great personalities who established organizations of national and international importance to generate human values like the Philosophy of Aurbindo, Ramana Maharshi, Narayana Guru etc. The birth places of such great personalities or the places of their organizations which are called philanthropic places, attracts the tourists.

Thus there is a great scope for development of tourism in the places having any one of the above five components, areas having beautiful multipurpose projects such as Dam, can also become areas of great interest for tourists.

Unfortunately most of the developing countries seem to believe that the answer to the problem is to establish public sector tourist enterprises. Tourism being a service industry, the key to its success is good management. This is precisely the area where public sector tourist establishments have generally proved to be less efficient. Part of the reason is that, historically tourism in the third world has not grown from grass roots as it did in Europe. In the developing countries, the process was reversed from the top downwards. The government, generally at the federal or central level, took the initiative in promoting tourism and its base gradually widened embracing the provincial municipal administrations. Private enterprise was associated with government efforts somewhat grudgingly, or was allowed to play a subservient role.

However, with the growth of international and even the domestic holiday market, the tourist industry, e.g. hoteliers, travel agents and ground tour operators have started asserting themselves, though not quite successfully because the carriers, airlines, railways and road transport services are usually owned and operated by the state. In some relatively less developed countries presumably the state had not alternative but to develop tourism in the public sector or invite foreign investors and operators to do the job. But in developing countries with a mixed economy and an enterprising and relatively well-developed private sector, governments had the alternative of allowing private enterprise to play its role by creating a favorable environment for investment and management.

Another fundamental question to which is developing country must find its own answer is: how much and what sort of tourism should a developing country cater for? The answer would be that for all developing countries some international tourism is desirable. Developing countries with large natural resources may have other equally viable alternatives available to them, but for those which have poor resources for economic development a high level of international tourism may be the best option for developing countries.

References

Bhatia, A.K. Tourism in India, Sterling Publications Pvt. Ltd., New

Delhi, 1978.

Bhatia, A.K. Tourism in India, Sterling Publishers Pvt. Ltd., New Delhi, 1978.

Dharmarajan, S., and Aviation, S. Tourism: a close linkage, *Yojana*, Vol. 40, No. 8, 1996.

Economic Impact, No. 29, International Communication Agency, Washington, D.C., USA, 1989/1, pp. 34-37.

Hugh and Colleen Gantzer. Tourism 2000: The great white hope, The Hindu Magazine, Sunday, January 8, 1995.

Leo's notes. Burst of activity in Tourism sector. The Hindu, Friday, December 22, 1995.

Likorish, L.J. and Kershaw, A.G. The Travel Trade, London, Practical Press, 1958.

Special Correspondent – Tourist arrivals go up, The Hindu, January 9, 1995.

Index

Index